Love Skills You Were Never Taught

Praise for Love Skills

"Spiritual, yet enormously practical at the same time."
  Deepak Chopra, Author, Peace is the Way

"The number one desire in our lives is to be loved – and this book shows you how."
  Arun Gandhi, Founder/President
  M. K. Gandhi Institute for Nonviolence

"**Love Skills You Were Never Taught** unpacks the mystery of love. Anyone can open this book & immediately learn these valuable love skills. The Pecks reveal how simple & clear love can be."
  Jack Canfield, Co-author,
  Chicken Soup for The Romantic Soul

"The Pecks have created a soon to be classic work that inspires the world towards healing, peace, & experiencing the Love we were all meant to share. They have splendidly succeeded in gathering 60 simple, practical, effective skills on giving and receiving love that will help love flow continuously throughout your life and into the lives of those you love."
  Gerald G. Jampolsky, M.D. & Diane V. Cirincione,
  Ph.D. Authors, Love is the Answer &
  Change Your Mind, Change Your Life

"This beautiful little book is like an ageless balm that soothes and enhances all relationships. Because they feel the divine pulse, the Pecks truly have their finger on the pulse of human love!"
  Stephen R. Covey, Author,
  The 7 Habits of Highly Effective People &
  The 8th Habit: From Effectiveness to Greatness

"**Love Skills You Were Never Taught** should be required reading for everyone over age twelve. I am grateful to Scott & Shannon Peck for tirelessly sharing their messages of love. They make the world a better place."
  Arielle Ford, Author,
  Hot Chocolate For The Mystical Soul

"Your ability to feel & express love is the key to joy in your life. This book shows you how to do it!"
Brian Tracy, Author, The Power of Charm

"What a treasure! This ground-breaking book doesn't just deliver – it transforms the reader! Every page is filled with practical ideas & rare spiritual insights that teach by example. Scott & Shannon are two Love Masters through & through. Their own lives & their incredible relationship is their most convincing testimony of all!"
Diana Loomans, Author,
What All Children Want Their Parents to Know

"Finally, the perfect book to teach love to anyone. Scott & Shannon Peck are the Masters of Love. The love skills in this book will bring forth the joy, passion, & prosperity of your soul."
Helice "Sparky" Bridges, Founder,
Difference Makers International,
Author, Who I Am Makes A Difference.

"**Love Skills You Were Never Taught** is a work of spiritual genius! Very few books grow on me the way **Love Skills** has, and most of those books are sacred texts or books of precious and delicious spiritual nectar. THANK YOU again and again and again for writing this book."
Russ Phelps,
Marketing Consultant/Copywriter

"Learning these love skills will change the way you look at life & interact in the universe. Love is the only game in town. Practice love, live love, be love. Read this book & become a Love Master. I did! I am!"
Bradley L. Winch Ph.D., J.D.
Co-author, Chicken Soup for the Soul:
Stories for a Better World

"Scott and Shannon Peck have written a wise book about the intricacies of intimate relationships. The skills they describe will help anyone find greater fulfillment & passion in life."
Larry Dossey, M.D., Author,
The Extraordinary Healing Power of Ordinary Things

"**Love Skills** unlocks the world of love. Readers will find themselves thinking, 'Now I understand how to create love on the spot & be a Love Master.'"

> **Dr. Angelo Pizelo**, President,
> Emerson Theological Institute

"Scott & Shannon write from their direct experience as Love Masters, generously sharing their skills for the benefit of all those who desire to awaken & experience their own heart of love."

> **Dr. Michael Bernard Beckwith**,
> Founder, Agape International Spiritual Center

"**Love Skills You Were Never Taught** is a helpful reminder of things you're almost embarrassed to think you need to be reminded of, but you do."

> **Marianne Williamson**, Author, The Gift of Change:
> Spiritual Guidance for a Radically New Life

"**Love Skills You Were Never Taught** provides an extraordinarily relevant & meaningful set of love skills to create & sustain a long term, intimate love relationship. Beyond that, the Pecks voice a cosmology of healing, attunement, well being, & spiritual awareness that we so need to re-balance our competitive, aggressive world.

> **Reverend Will Newsom**,
> Church of Today, San Diego, California

"What touches me most is the *tone* of this book. I have the impression you are reading it out loud to me, with your arms resting gently on my shoulders. Thank you for being that beacon of Love sending out light all round the world."

> **Pierre Pradervand**, Author
> The Gentle Art of Blessing

"You can ascend your God Ladder with these powerful love skills. They will strengthen your spiritual muscles and open your heart. Prepare for a love infusion!"

> **Dr. Judith Larkin Reno**, President Gateway
> University, Author, A Mystic's View of War:
> Using the God Ladder for Clarity

"These **Love Skills**, conscientiously assimilated into everyday situations – lived & felt from the heart – carry the power of planetary transformation. The use of these love skills translates ultimately into world peace & justice for all. These finely tuned and comprehensive love skills unite individual consciousness with the divine."

    Tom Russell, Retired Judge

"This book is so valuable! The lessons in this book provide wonderful opportunities to share with others and see for ourselves the Love Master that exists within each of us. I'll be recommending this to all who study with me."

    William M. Heller, Teacher, A Course in Miracles

"**Love Skills You Were Never Taught** can be used with psychotherapy clients to discover relationship skills that they never learned. The Pecks offer practical & easy-to-understand concepts that can be used to guide people through the process of creating, maintaining, & enhancing healthy, loving relationships."

    Julieann Myers, LCSW, CACIII, MAC, Licensed
    clinical social worker, nationally-recognized trainer,
    psychotherapist, coach, & addictions specialist

"**Love Skills You Were Never Taught** speaks to everyone seeking higher love. Rather than giving techniques, the Pecks show how to practice and live the precious talents of love in your own life."

    Dr. Pietro Grieco, Author, The Boy & the Prophet

"Who was ever taught the skills of love? Most of us have had to learn love the hard way. **Love Skills** is a handbook for a life filled with the poetry of loving. Shannon & Scott Peck offer valuable guidance in love – page after page!"

    Dessa Byrd Reed, Poet & Author,
    The Butterfly Touch & Seven Bridges

"What is more important than developing love skills? The Pecks help us eliminate trial & error & practice love so that we can become Love Masters. Great book. Everyone can benefit!"

    Dr. Thom A. Lisk, CEO, TerrificSpeakers.com

Also by Scott & Shannon Peck

The Love You Deserve
A Spiritual Guide to Genuine Love

Liberating Your Magnificence
Opening Your Life to Infinite Possibilities

Love Heals
How to Heal Everything with Love
by Shannon Peck

Love Heals Study Guide
by Shannon Peck

Love Skills
You Were Never
Taught

Secrets of a Love Master

Dr. Scott Peck
Shannon Peck

Love Skills You Were Never Taught
Secrets of a Love Master
Copyright © 2015 by Scott & Shannon Peck
Revised, Second Edition

LifePath Publishing
1127 Santa Luisa Solana Beach CA 92075

Cover by Robert Howard
Cover painting by Lindsay Duff
Printed by Amazon CreateSpace

ISBN-13: 978-0692502846 (Lifepath Publishing)
ISBN-10: 069250284X

Publisher's Cataloging-in-Publication
(Provided by Quality Books, Inc.)

Peck, Scott,
   Love skills You Were Never Taught:
secrets of a love master / by Scott & Shannon Peck.
   p. cm.
   ISBN-10: 069250284X
   1. Love--Handbooks, manuals, etc. 2. Interpersonal relations--Handbooks, manuals, etc. 3. Intimacy (Psychology) 4. Spiritual life.   I. Peck, Shannon.
II. Title. III. Title: love skills you were never traught.

BF575.L8P4 2006   158.2
                        QBI05-600218

*This book is dedicated
to the
Love Master
within you*

Love Master: A person highly skilled in loving. Specifically, someone who demonstrates a high level of love awareness & expertise in creating love through a multitude of love skills, including living in Love alignment, loving oneself, greeting others with love, creating intimacy, expanding love, creating peace, healing with love, & leaving a trail of love when parting.

Table of Contents

Greeting Others With Love

Creating Intimacy

Expanding Love

Creating Peace

Healing with Love

Leaving A Trail of Love

Appendix

Living Your Life as a Love Master

There is a great love awakening taking place and this awakening is both personal and global. Quite simply, we are all being called by Love, the highest power in the universe, to usher in the Age of Love. Love wants each of us to be activated as a Love Master and fulfill our highest love destiny.

As our lives accelerate in our advancing civilization, the number one thing we most want in life has never changed. We want to be loved. Yet the gap between our desire for love and our actual experience of love is enormous. We have not been taught love well. When was the last time you took a course in becoming a love expert or upgraded your love skills from "Basic Love" to "Advanced Love?"

It is time for the great suffering from lack of love to end on Earth, and to allow Love to re-create us. This is a moment to pause and envision what is possible for us as Love beings. The old way of experiencing love is dissolving. Higher consciousness offers a new way of knowing ourselves as Love beings skilled in the use of transforming love skills.

Love is reaching into our hearts and lifting us to a new view of what is possible in love – a vast new love story awakening us all to the "Age of Love." It is from this core place that this book is written.

This is such a new and transforming dimension of love that we need a new name to describe who we are becoming – and that name is **Love Master**.

Just as concert masters, web masters, or Zen masters demonstrate mastery in their areas of expertise, a Love Master demonstrates mastery in creating love.

> **Love Master:** A person highly skilled in loving. Specifically, someone who demonstrates a high level of love awareness & expertise in creating love through a multitude of love skills, including living in Love alignment, loving oneself, greeting others with love, creating intimacy, expanding love, creating peace, healing with love, & leaving a trail of love when parting.

We have all been touched by Love Masters. Whenever you are being cherished, esteemed, empowered, and honored by another person, you are in the presence of a Love Master. Whenever you are expressing these qualities, then you are living as a Love Master yourself.

Our world needs Love Masters in every home, school, job, and organization. Imagine the quality of our world if we were all Love Masters! Imagine how fulfilling your life would be if you knew and practiced the skills of a Love Master. Well, now you can.

You can only rise as high in love as you can conceive – so look deeply into the heart and vision of a Love Master as you read on and prepare to take your invaluable place in the Age of Love.

The Sacred Questions of a Love Master

Rather than acting from the old paradigm of wondering, *"How can I find or get more love?"* the sacred question inside the heart of a Love Master is a new one and it exudes the energy of healing: *"How loved do you feel in my presence?"*

This new view of living our lives as the Presence of Love changes everything. By practicing being the Presence of Love, we allow Love to permeate and flow through us and spill out to others. Love knows how to make itself known. Everyone feels it. Living as the Presence of Love unifies and connects hearts and brings transformation – both personally and globally.

Think of the persons you most love – your love mate, children, friends, and family members. Do they feel the Presence of Love when they are with you?

Think of all the people at your workplace, your organizations, the stores you visit, and all the people you pass in life. Do they feel the Presence of Love when you pass through their lives?

As a Love Master, you relish being the Presence of Love to everyone – all the time. That's what this book is about. It will teach you, or help you refine, the love skills that enable you to live as the very Presence of Love.

One morning, at breakfast with a good friend, a waitress we knew and loved took our order with a smile and then left. We thought to ourselves, "Something is not right in her life." When she later came by, we asked her if she would sit with us for a moment. "What did I do wrong?" she said. "Nothing at all," we said with great compassion. "We were just having fun identifying the two words that best describe who we are at our core level and we wanted to include you. What would be the two words that best describe your essence?"

She responded instantly with a big smile: "My words would be loving and witty." As she shared so easily from her heart, her entire body and identity relaxed in the love that was embracing her. She was reminded of how magnificent she is. She told us she was going through a rough time and our short time together had lifted her heart immensely. She only sat with us for 60 seconds, but she left our table transformed, invigorated, and loved.

That's just a small example of what happens when we embrace others as Love Masters – using such love skills as *Tuning in to Another's Heart*, *Asking Love Questions*, and *Listening with Empathy*.

Becoming a Love Master creates a powerful flow of love that nourishes others, enriches our own soul, and attracts the most loving people to us. In fact, the fastest way to meet the right love mate is to become a Love Master. It may seem like a paradox – because a Love Master seeks to give, not receive. But it is really the most profound of spiritual laws – loving well brings you into the heart of all Love.

Living from the sacred space of *"How loved do you feel in my presence?"* creates a powerful wave of love, joy, and healing in your life.

Just as illuminating is another question that each of us, as Love Masters, learns to ask as we interact with others. *"How loved do I feel by others?"* This question causes us to become aware of whether we are feeling the presence of love as well.

There are thousands of loving people right now who are giving massive amounts of love and receiving little or none in return. This is not the love they deserve. Genuine love flows equally in both directions. As we grow in our understanding of what it means to become a Love Master, we discover the vast importance of being surrounded by people who honor and empower us – who help us see our deep value to the world. In other words, to be surrounded by Love Masters. You deserve to feel the Presence of Love flowing to you just as much as it flows from you.

As Love Masters, we also need to love ourselves – just as well as we would love our best friend. Unconditional and universal love are concepts deeply embedded in the heart of a Love Master and both these terms include everyone – including you. Loving yourself richly is a big part of the awakening to the immensely fulfilling life of a Love Master.

How loved do others feel in your presence? How loved do you feel by others? And how well do you love yourself? These three questions, combined, may shake the foundations of your entire life, but these are the questions shaping the new Age of Love.

The easiest way to answer these questions with fulfillment is to practice living the 60 love skills of a Love Master. And what a life this is! Are you ready for a truly love-centered life – a life flowing out with love and also receiving love's fullness? This is the love you deserve. This is the new love story for our civilization.

What It's Like to Live as a Love Master

Becoming a Love Master shifts love to an entirely new context. You become aware of the vast importance of love in your everyday life and events. Your highest Love Self is activated!

As you learn and practice these 60 transforming love skills, you will become fluent in the language of love!

You will quickly find yourself **Moving into Love Alignment** – seeing yourself as the very Presence of Love – and living from this consciousness.

As you practice being the Presence of Love as a Love Master, you will discover the joy of **Loving Yourself** which includes *Receiving Love Generously, Cherishing Your Life Purpose, Seeing Yourself as a Masterpiece, Setting Boundaries,* and *Forgiving Yourself.*

You will rejoice in the simple love skills that cause others to immediately feel the vast energy of Love's Presence as you practice **Greeting Others with Love**.

You will become an expert and at ease in **Creating Intimacy** and **Expanding Love** with more than 20 powerful love skills, such as: *Asking Love Questions, Listening with Empathy, Reflecting Back & Validating, Honoring Soul, Facilitating Equality, Cherishing Dreams,* and *Creating Unity.*

You will learn how to **Create Peace** with a multitude of love skills that dissolve conflict into peace, such as: *Envisioning Peace, Setting in Motion a Peace Process, Getting Feelings Out, Being a Loving but Detached Observer, Exploring Solutions for Unity & Justice,* and *Creating a Peace Ending.*

The final destination of love is healing. You will bring powerful healing to yourself and others as you practice the eight illuminating love skills of **Healing with Love** which include: *Asking Love, Speaking as Love, Calling*

Forth the Divine, Offering Sweet Assurance, Resonating with Love, and *Holding the Space for Healing.*

Living as a Love Master, you can expect richer relationships and greater appreciation of who you are – from others and yourself. You can expect a more expansive life fulfillment and inner guidance from Love that will enable you to be an amazing blessing to everyone in your life.

As a Love Master, your life will also have a planetary healing effect. A Love Master's lover is all humanity.

You become more awake and responsive to the immense suffering on Earth – the tears in so many million hearts, the private inner struggles for worth and purpose, and the catastrophic, often hidden, results of anguish and abuse. Your inner heart as a Love Master feels all this and responds vigorously and powerfully to this universal call for help.

Your use of the love skills of a Love Master will also awaken other Love Masters who are ready for love and eager to interact at a soul level. Your living as the Presence of Love will also result in the right love mate, friends, and communities. You will find yourself *Resonating in Love* in every dimension of your life.

Every step towards becoming a Love Master unleashes new powers of Love within you. Please see and acknowledge your magnificence as Love's Presence. Your Love Master Self is qualified to be Love's Universal Champion! As you read this book, you will understand how to take your destined place as a Love Master in the Age of Love!

> With infinite Love,
> Scott & Shannon Peck

How to Use this Book

Each of the 60 love skills in this book stands alone as a love skill with immense power. To help your learning be quick and clear, we have presented each love skill in just two pages – along with a self-quiz question so you can evaluate yourself with each skill. The full 60-question Love Skills Quiz is in the back of the book.

The 60 love skills are grouped into eight families to help you see how these skills work together in real life:

1. Grounding Yourself in Love
2. Loving Yourself
3. Greeting Others with Love
4. Creating Intimacy
5. Expanding Love
6. Creating Peace
7. Healing with Love
8. Leaving a Trail of Love

There are many ways to use this book to advance your love skills. You can, of course, just read this book from cover to cover. It moves swiftly.

This is a great book, however, to read randomly. Just let your inspiration or curiosity lead you to the love skills you most want to know more about.

As you practice the 60 love skills and reread this book often, you will gain an increasingly refined sense of the amazing power of each love skill. You will also discover the extraordinary power of combining any two or more love skills together – simultaneously.

Whenever faced with a love challenge – in a relationship, at work, with family, with friends, or within your own heart – quietly identify which of the 60 love skills would most bring healing to the situation. We do this often ourselves.

You will be surprised how this practice of love awareness brings swift answers and raises your love consciousness to new, higher levels.

To advance to the highest possibilities as a Love Master, you can identify which love skills you are currently weakest at living and decide to become an expert with these specific skills. Take your list with you and look at them often through the day. A simple reminder of the skills on your list will help bring you into a greater love awareness and fulfillment.

We have created beautiful, laminated 4x6 inspiration cards for each love skill (see appendix) which is another way to make this easy. Many people put one of the attractive love skills cards at their desk or bed to remind them to live this love skill.

This is a great book to leave out in the open in your home so you can have easy love inspiration and immediate, practical application.

Sharing this book with others is also a great conversation starter for genuine love talk and a perfect way to practice the love skills yourself of taking the initiative to create more intimacy.

This is also a great book for teaching love skills to others – family, kids, friends, co-workers, or groups. One fun & light way to do this is to play the "Love Skills" game. This is an excellent method for learning the love skills in an entertaining way.

Here's one way to play:

One person acts out a love skill and the other(s) try to guess which love skill it is. One big benefit of this love game is that everyone wins. Even if you guess wrong, you are identifying ways the other person is expressing love! This teaches how overlapping and simultaneous these love skills are in real life and how powerful they are when fused together.

So welcome again to the life of a Love Master. We hope you enjoy this book – in many ways and for a long time!

Grounding Yourself in Love

*Love Alignment
is the
deepest inner secret
of a
Love Master*

1

Move Into

Love Alignment

When you move into Love alignment,

you become one with your

Highest Self

Love alignment is the deepest inner secret of a Love Master and gives you full capacity to live all 60 love skills at a 10 (on a scale from 1 to 10).

Think of Love as a Higher Power, a divine Presence, and the Source from which all love originates and flows. This is what you align yourself with as a Love Master.

In Love alignment, you think, feel, speak, and act as Love itself – the universal force of compassion, healing, and unity. Envision this as a description of you. Love flows through you so thoroughly that it would be more accurate to say that Love is expressing Itself *as* you.

Love alignment brings astounding results. You feel centered in your highest possible selfhood. You know you are drawing from the Highest Source. Others feel the presence of Love when they are with you.

And here's the wonderful news. Love alignment is easy. It requires only your desire and decision to enter this high place of a Love Master.

Would you like to experience this right now?

We'll help you.

Find a quiet place to be alone. As you sit quietly, let the

rest of the world fall away. Become aware of your breathing and let this be your doorway into universal Love. With each inhale, imagine Love filling you. With each exhale, release all negative feelings and thoughts. Do this slowly for about a dozen rounds of breathing. As you relax and surrender in this process, you will be infused with Love. You will feel yourself moving into Love alignment. Love was there all along.

Now gently shift the focus of your exhale. Keep filling up with Love with each inhale, and now, with each exhale, let Love pour out into the universe to touch those you love, those you are struggling with, and all those in the universe who need love. As you sit in this place, consider this your home base. Notice how it makes you feel. Spending moments in Love alignment each day will affect you deeply and in many ways.

The beauty of using breath to tune in to Love is that you are always breathing. Take advantage of this most natural rhythm, always available, to tune in to Love.

As you continue tuning in to Love, let Love wash through your entire being – your thinking, feeling, and seeing. Feel Love's peace fill your heart. Open yourself in surrender and humility to Love. Feel yourself coming into even deeper Love alignment.

Love alignment is an invisible love skill and a private experience between you and Love. It is from this sacred place of oneness with Love that all the skills of a Love Master flow into your being, not as technique, but as you practice being the Presence of Love.

Love Skills Quiz

Love flows through me as I think, feel,
speak, & act...

1	2	3	4	5	6	7	8	9	10
Never		Seldom		Sometimes			Often		Always

Loving

Yourself

Loving yourself
allows you
to receive
all that Love
has in store
for you

#2

Receive Love Generously

*Receiving love generously
calls you to open your heart & life
to all the gifts waiting for you from Love*

How open are you to receiving love generously? We encourage you to open your heart to all that Love wants you to experience.

Loving people often find it easier to love others more than themselves, but this is not Love's way. Love is universal. It embraces everyone fully – and that includes you! Loving yourself is part of Love's wonderful plan for your life.

Loving yourself is not about ego or selfishness. It is about opening yourself to receive all the gifts that Love wants for you. You deserve to feel worthy within. You deserve relationships that genuinely honor your being. You deserve to flow through life with inner confidence. You deserve to like – and yes, love – yourself. We all deserve this.

Consider how much pleasure you as a Love Master have in giving love. It is just as important for others to have this same opportunity to give love to you. This requires that you let yourself receive their love.

How can you do this?

Notice when someone else is giving love to you – by their words or actions. Then notice what you do as a response. Do you push their giving away? Hurry them to finish and be through? Interrupt? Or say to yourself, or aloud, "That's enough," even before they are finished?

As you become increasingly aware of how you resist receiving love generously, you will create a new habit of being a happy recipient – a generous recipient!

Since giving is good for the soul, you, as a Love Master, notice and even encourage generous love-giving to you. By your gracious, open receiving of love from others, you also encourage them to stay in the flow of love.

When you receive love generously, there is a second benefit to everyone. You create more intimacy. It may feel that you are being more vulnerable to receive love so openly and generously, but rather than viewing this as a weakness, think of this as a strength of being more transparent, more visible, and more centered in love. Transparency draws hearts closer together.

Welcome to this life-defining Love moment. Love is inviting you to experience all that Love has in store for you. Do you accept Love's invitation? We hope you do.

Loving yourself means you let the presence of Love flow to you at all times. It means you have full permission to receive all love and enjoy it without any feelings of guilt. It means you accept continuous self-nurturing, comfort, and encouragement as always available and never withheld. It means you genuinely like and love *you*! Thank you for receiving our love so generously right now.

Thank you for accepting Love's invitation. You are taking a giant step forward as a Love Master.

Love Skills Quiz

I receive love generously...

1	2	3	4	5	6	7	8	9	10
Never		Seldom		Sometimes			Often		Always

#3

Cherish

Your Life Purpose

You are alive to know & fulfill your highest purpose in life

Why are you here on earth? What is your reason for being? What are the gifts you have come here to share? What is your destiny?

These wonderful questions deserve to be answered within your soul as part of loving your magnificent, core self.

There is a mission within you, deeply encoded, and yearning to be known and expressed. Listen to the intuitive voice within you as you consider what makes your heart sing.

- What are you most passionate about?
- What is most important to your heart?
- What is being called forth within you to be gifted to the universe?

Considering the highest possibilities for your life causes your magnificence to awaken. This is how to cherish your life purpose.

Your life purpose is more than what you occupy as a job. It is who you are and becoming. It is the character you are developing and being. It is the values you practice in your relationships and actions. It is your motives and decisions. It is the positive effect you have on others. Life purpose comes from your pure inner light, directing your entire life. Your life purpose is constantly evolving. As you contemplate this, you will discover even more of your true self and open with more clarity to your life purpose.

Your life purpose isn't about money, status, power, or recognition you receive. It is about knowing your deepest desires and living closely to them as you continue to learn more about them.

Such living weaves a beautiful web of connectedness to others on the same path of highest self exploration. It creates a sense of richness and inner peace entirely beyond what the world can give you. It ultimately becomes your contribution to all creation. This is how you fit in with everything in life. And it's a beautiful fit, worthy of your generous love.

You and your Source are the only authority on the subject of your life purpose. Others cannot tell you what it is. You are the one holding the key to your vast magnificence.

As you live your life and learn to love yourself at a richer level, remind yourself constantly:

I am here for a wonderful purpose. As I tune in to know more, my purpose quietly speaks to me so that I can sense what steps to take. My purpose is woven into even the smallest areas of my life. Nothing is insignificant. As I honor and cherish this process, all life's blessings open up to reveal more of who I am and what I am doing here. Everything becomes more beautiful and meaningful because I am loving my Highest Self and my reason for being alive.

Love Skills Quiz

I know & cherish my life purpose...

1	2	3	4	5	6	7	8	9	10
Never		Seldom		Sometimes			Often		Always

33

#4

Create Sacred
Time Alone

*Sacred solitude
creates stillness for
inspiration & healing*

Creating sacred time to be alone with yourself and Love, or your Highest Power, is a powerful and nurturing way of loving yourself.

In quietness and stillness, you can listen to your heart, reflect on your life, and receive guidance from the Highest Source, Love. In stillness, you find higher answers to your struggles. You get to know yourself more deeply and clearly. You experience peace.

Allow yourself to experience this right now.

As you create the opportunity for solitude, don't worry about what to do. Simply enjoy the gift of this sacred moment. Use it to cherish yourself with tenderness and openness.

Set aside thoughts about all that is taking place in your life. Let stillness come into your heart. Be free of all judgment of yourself or others. Let go of what anyone thinks about you and how that affects you.

Let your heart open to its most reverent and highest place. Quietly accept into your thinking only thoughts that come to you directly from your Highest Self. Release your mind's busyness and listen to your Source. Let Love flow through your entire being.

Be open to the presence of Love speaking in your heart with reassurance and insight. The realization of Truth dawns quietly in stillness.

Begin to reflect on your life, giving yourself generous opportunity to be present and open with your thoughts and feelings in a peaceful way. In this quietness, remember who you are and offer yourself generous love.

In this healing atmosphere, you may pull out your entire list of what needs to be healed – within yourself, with others, and with those who need your help – and listen for guidance.

Or you may find your thought turning to the world's needs and offering compassion.

Or you may just enjoy the peace of the stillness.

It is not so important what happens in your sacred time alone, but that you experience this soul-soothing quietness frequently.

Daily moments of even short sacred solitude are enormously healing. The guidance and inspiration that unfold during these times of quietness uplift your spirit and enable you to walk into life more invigorated and with greater clarity, focus, balance, and compassion.

Taking time alone is not selfish – any more than eating for nourishment is selfish.

Sacred stillness is a soul necessity and giant way of loving yourself generously.

Love Skills Quiz

I give myself sacred solitude so I can be still & listen to Love (or Higher Power) for guidance...

1	2	3	4	5	6	7	8	9	10
Never		Seldom		Sometimes			Often		Always

#5

Honor & Speak Your Feelings

*Honoring your feelings is
healing to your heart*

Do you know what you are feeling at this moment? Do you speak up and share your feelings?

When you honor your feelings, you come to your own aid with empowerment. Listening to your feelings gives you information that helps resolve inner struggles and needs. Without knowing your feelings, you neglect a basic need that enables you to be happy and free.

Habitually stuffing down feelings leads to a practice of low self esteem. It sends a message that you and your feelings are not important or worthy of being known.

Have you ever been told by someone, "You shouldn't feel that way?" There is no "should" in feelings. Feelings simply are.

Rather than being defined by your feelings, look at your feelings from a point of observation and learn about yourself. Feelings are interesting. They tell us when we feel fear, anger, hurt, guilt, sadness, shame, and when we feel like crying. They tell us how we view ourselves. They also help us identify what makes us feel touched, joyful, optimistic, glad, calm, free, grateful, relieved, and proud.

There are millions of feelings! How many can you identify right now? Can you feel your feelings – negative or positive – without fear? Can you give yourself permission to look at your feelings regardless of others' opinions?

Honoring your feelings means that you are open to knowing them. And open to speaking up to honor them.

Some feelings are so overwhelming that it may take courage to face them. Once faced, however, they can receive your love and honoring. Some of us have been conditioned to think that certain feelings are wrong. We feel ashamed for even feeling them! So we accept the false belief that when those feelings arise, they should be ignored and left unexamined.

We all suffer from not knowing our feelings. Without knowing and honoring your own feelings, and without speaking up, your actions will fail to represent you and often confuse others. By daring to look at negative feelings within, you see how much pain they are causing you.

By honoring your feelings, you allow them to surface so that you can know yourself and honor yourself more openly. You discover how to make better decisions and create new habits that free you. You learn how to speak your feelings in a loving way. Healing emerges – even physical healing.

A wonderful way of discovering your feelings is through journaling. This helps you discover the power of identifying and validating your feelings and allowing no one else to tell you what you are feeling, or that your feelings are wrong. Journaling lets you speak up – to yourself.

Love yourself by listening to your feelings, honoring them, and validating your right to feel what is within.

Love Skills Quiz

I honor, validate, & speak my feelings...

1	2	3	4	5	6	7	8	9	10
Never		Seldom		Sometimes			Often		Always

#6

See Yourself As a Masterpiece

*Think of yourself
as Love's beautiful, unfolding
masterpiece*

You are a masterpiece in progress. Michelangelo left unfinished works of enormous raw slabs of marble with beautiful images emerging. These masterpieces were already evident though the works were unfinished.

Think of yourself as Love's emerging Masterpiece! You are being carved out, shaped, and formed by your life experiences, relationships, values, and choices, but you are already exquisitely beautiful right now!

And you are becoming even more wonderful as you chisel out higher ways of loving.

It is so easy to see ourselves as unworthy. Living in self rejection and self judgment means you deny yourself joy, passion, dreaming, and self expression. Rather than depriving yourself of the self love you deserve, give yourself support, acknowledgment, encouragement, and praise. You are worthy.

If you find that you can easily accept others without negative judgment, yet struggle to accept yourself, practice becoming an expert at both.

One way you can practice this love skill is by journaling.

In a simple notebook, journal what you did today that you liked. Let this self-love feeling sink in. Notice how this new energy feels. Let your heart and mind explore all the new circuitry to find this place of acceptance again and again. You are beginning a new habit of watching yourself rise higher and giving yourself credit.

In this same journal, notice your new, positive inner talk. At first it may seem awkward, but your goal is to accept yourself without negative judgment and allow this to become a natural way of living and regarding yourself.

Practice constructive self judgment where you objectively look at your life to make better choices. Just as scientists in the laboratory observe an experiment to learn more, objectively look at any negative areas of your life to learn more. Rather than looking at your life as moments of pain or failure and beating yourself up, use your energy to learn and grow towards healing solutions.

Let self evaluation be a positive learning experience rather than an opportunity to say, "I can't do anything right! I hate myself!" Learn to love yourself even as you are changing and evolving.

Learn to look at yourself as a beautiful work of art and with grand approval. Experience the happiness of seeing yourself as the *best you* so far!

Practice getting good at accepting yourself. Look deep within and continuously acknowledge:

"I may make mistakes, but I am beautiful within my heart and I am becoming even more beautiful as I continue learning and growing. I see and love myself as Love's masterpiece in progress."

Love Skills Quiz

I see & love myself as a masterpiece unfolding ...

1	2	3	4	5	6	7	8	9	10
Never		Seldom		Sometimes			Often		Always

7

Practice
Inner Love Talk

The practice of positive inner love talk
creates peace, joy, & self-esteem

Positive inner love talk is a rich way to love yourself. As you let positive love talk flow steadily through your thinking, you are letting the voice of Love remind you continuously that you are valuable and lovable.

It's easy to rehearse negative things all day long – how you fail to compare well with others, your inadequacies, fears, insecurities, and inferiorities. This becomes a habit and it develops inner sadness and mediocrity.

You have a choice, however, to practice a far better habit of positive inner love talk and watch your joy and productivity increase dramatically.

For example, at the end of each day, review privately the top three things you most loved about yourself that day. What did you do best? What was your best moment of thinking? What was your highest action?

Such positive inner love talk breaks the habit of negative, recycling self talk. Let love talk take the stage in your steady flow of inner thinking so you can experience greater freedom, relaxation, and happiness. Your life will open more easily to the realm of higher possibilities.

Here are more questions to help you create positive inner love talk:

- What did I do today that was hard, but I did it well?
- How did I love someone well today?
- What did I learn today?

Productive questions like these generate positive inner love talk and growth. And this habit will beautifully support and sustain you in hard times.

When you practice inner love talk, you are re-creating your automatic response to every situation. The outcome is deeply stabilizing for more joy and greater equilibrium.

Another way to practice inner love talk is to develop inner talk headlines that affirm your worth and then hit the play button repeatedly. For example:

- Love is with me.
- I am growing steadily in my love skills.
- I am Love's golden light of beauty.
- My life carries great value.

Congratulate yourself repeatedly for every positive private thought you have about yourself and watch your energy grow. When negative talk begins again, don't cave in to a re-run of old tapes. Replace them with these new and positive tapes of inner love for yourself.

You control the play button so practice being your top love advocate. Everyone makes mistakes and can learn from their mistakes, including you. Give yourself the benefit of doubt when your old habit sucks you back down. Release it and let yourself soar once again into the inner love space you deserve.

The practice of positive inner love talk creates peace, joy, & self esteem and is a powerful way to love yourself.

Love Skills Quiz

I practice positive inner love talk as a healthy way of loving myself well...

1	2	3	4	5	6	7	8	9	10
Never		Seldom		Sometimes			Often		Always

#8

Love
Your Body

Your body is your vehicle

for expressing love

& fulfilling your highest purpose

Your body is of utmost importance to fulfilling your highest reason for being alive.

We are conditioned to think of our physical bodies with great negative judgment. Take a higher step in loving yourself by laying aside judgment as you consider new and higher views of your body.

Your life needs a vehicle for expressing love and your Highest Selfhood – your reason for coming to Earth. This vehicle is your body and it fulfills an enormous purpose in this lifetime.

Seeing your body as your prime vehicle for loving and giving your great riches enables you to view your body with great appreciation. From this highest point of view, you see the natural wisdom of cherishing and respecting your body. Your body needs your love to fulfill its mission.

There is a tendency to compare yourself with other bodies and wish you were taller, slimmer, or better looking. Vanity puts us in a place of self criticism and dissatisfaction. Our culture conditions us to view our shape or size as unacceptable, even disappointing. We

can spend an entire lifetime hating our nose, complexion, thighs, or stomach. We act as our own worst enemy. Such comparisons make us slaves to a superficial view of life that misses the entire point of our reason for being.

Loving your body does not mean you won't work to improve your body or looks. Exercise, yoga, balanced, nourishing eating, the practice of good health care, and plenty of rest are intelligent ways of loving your body and enabling your body to fulfill your life mission. You can do all these things with love, not self-hate. This is an essential part of your practice of loving yourself.

Your body is worthy of being cherished and loved just as it is – a wonderful vehicle allowing you to become all you were destined to be and enabling you to express and experience all the love that is in store for you.

Get to know your real body. Your real body is what you embody. Go past your physical appearance and make a list of the qualities you most embody.

- What are your top five qualities?
- What are the top five reasons your closest friends love you?
- What role does your physical body play in fulfilling your wonderful life mission?

This is your real body. This is the body others see when they say, "I love you." You are beautiful!

Thank your body for carrying you around in a state of being alive. Thank your body for functioning so incredibly to enable you to explore the world, experience love, give love, and fulfill your life purpose. Thank your body for its endless willingness to support you.

Love your body with all the love it deserves!

Love Skills Quiz

I love my body & appreciate its value in
helping me fulfill my life purpose...

1	2	3	4	5	6	7	8	9	10
Never		Seldom		Sometimes			Often		Always

#9

Be Visible

Being visible allows the universe

to see & love the real you

How visible are you? How well do others know who you are? Do you reveal yourself fully to anyone?

We are not talking about revealing your innermost secrets or becoming loud, obnoxious, unloving, or blatant. We are talking about your lovely inner self and its fullest expression – your unique individuality revealed!

You are unduplicatable. There will never be another you. This is true for everyone who has ever lived or ever will live. Each of us is unique. Yet, rather than celebrating our uniqueness, we often strive to conform to each other.

Think of people you most admire for being fully visible. On a scale from 1 to 10, Monet was a 10 when he painted his water lilies, Beethoven was a 10 when he composed his 9th symphony, Ghandi was a 10 in living for non-violence. Oprah is a 10 continually. It takes courage and boldness to be who you are without hiding or timidity or being a watered-down version of yourself.

Why don't we just come forth?

There is a right of passage in becoming visible. In the hero's journey, there are dragons that must be slain in order to reach destiny. The dragons on the destiny path to visibility are fears of rejection, being judged when we expose ourselves, losing esteem, and even losing someone's love. We tell ourselves that we could lose.

Do we dare risk everything by being visible? After all,

we've invested a life in conforming so no one will notice our inner selves.

Everyone wants to find their soul mates and soul groups, but if no one is fully visible, how can we find each other?

There are many advantages to being visible. The value of knowing who you are means that no one else can tell you who you are. You are also less likely to be confused by someone's misunderstanding or false interpretation of you.

Being visible means that you access your inner self and are willing to share it with others. There is deep satisfaction in revealing your core self and its innate goodness and worth. Everyone is full of treasures beyond the superficial layers of timidness, fear, and defenses. Wouldn't you like to see more of these treasures in everyone, including yourself?

What would your fully visible, genuine self look like?

Practice taking one step forward today to be more visible. And another step forward tomorrow. Step by step, you will come to see who you are.

Be visible like flowers that don't hold back their vivid colors, fragrances, sizes, and beautiful shapes. We love them for their rich individuality.

This is how you deserve to be loved too!

Thank you for every step you take to be more visible in sharing your magnificence with the universe.

We need your visibility!

Love Skills Quiz

I am fully visible to myself and to others and I allow myself freedom to be me...

1	2	3	4	5	6	7	8	9	10
Never		Seldom		Sometimes			Often		Always

#10
Set
Boundaries

Setting healthy boundaries
honors your needs as just as important
as the needs of others

Setting boundaries gives you the opportunity to know and honor yourself without interference from others.

Setting boundaries is an opportunity to check in with yourself, without outside intrusion, to consider your own feelings, needs, desires, and choices. Are you free to feel your own feelings? Make your own decisions? Act in a way that honors your needs?

Here are some of the ways we fail to set boundaries.

You know you are allowing someone to infringe on your boundary line when you are feeling controlled through manipulation, domination, condemnation, or anger. Rather than your own needs or feelings being considered, these are being discounted and overlooked in favor of another person's wishes.

You also may be feeling pressured or rushed into something before you have had a chance to think it through.

Sometimes we willingly give away our power in our efforts to please others so they will love us in return.

Or, giving away our power may be a way we try to keep

peace in a relationship. We need to consider the price we pay when we allow our feelings, thoughts, or needs to be buried. Is numbing ourselves worth it?

Setting boundaries for yourself means that your needs are just as important as another's needs. As you reflect on your own needs or feelings in any given area of your life, you can then speak up in a loving and effective way.

Can you say "Yes" and mean it? Can you also say "No" and make it stick without feeling guilty? Can you set boundaries in a loving, kind way – even when you feel pressured? These are the refinements of a Love Master.

What if someone tried to sing your life's song for you? Or someone tried to drown out your song? Or by someone's insistence, you were never able to sing your song?

Each of these instances requires setting your boundaries. Look at it as a process of standing in your own light, not cowering, but prevailing with who you are and without dominating someone else's boundaries.

Maintaining a strong sense of identity and walking in your own shoes, you live in the love awareness that you are the only one who can best represent your unique self on earth.

Our diversity is beautiful! Each of our songs can be sung in infinitely unique ways and still be beautiful.

Setting boundaries creates the freedom we all need to sing our life songs.

How will you sing your song?

Love Skills Quiz

I set healthy boundaries that honor my needs
as just as important as other's needs...

1	2	3	4	5	6	7	8	9	10
Never		Seldom		Sometimes			Often		Always

#11

Forgive Yourself

Self-forgiveness
is an intelligent & enlightened way
of loving yourself

Forgiveness begins with an attitude towards life of acceptance and learning rather than condemnation and despair. You make a life choice not to condemn yourself but rather to appreciate all you are learning as you move higher.

For example, if you look at the human experience all the way from infancy to old age, you quickly understand that absolutely everyone is on a learning curve. We all make mistakes. Lots of them. The idea of perfection is unachievable.

What can you do about this?

You can practice self forgiveness as an intelligent and enlightened way of loving yourself.

Some things you learn easily and well in life. Other things are more difficult and come more slowly – and with mistakes.

Often, however, the most challenging areas of our lives, where we thought or acted at less than our highest possibility, teach us the most valuable lessons. Such "failures" cause us to grow in character and wisdom.

And we do grow. Think of what you were like 10 years ago compared to today. Congratulations for all you have learned!

By allowing yourself to make plenty of mistakes – without judging yourself for being stupid or wrong, you stay in a loving place with yourself. You see your mistakes as opportunities to learn rather than opportunities to condemn or hate yourself and you move forward in life.

Can you look at the past and release feelings of guilt, regret, and disappointment over what you said or did? Or what you failed to say or do but wish you had? Look at the areas where you have the most regret over past behaviors and start forgiving yourself right now.

Let your life have an attitude of humility as you choose to forgive yourself. We're all going to make more mistakes. As Henry Kissinger is reported to have said to his staff when taking over as Secretary of State: "We're not going to make the same old mistakes. We're going to make new mistakes." There is great wisdom in this humor.

By practicing self forgiveness, exchanging your self-condemning feelings with more honoring ones, you move towards a place of freedom and inner peace. Negative feelings will lessen and finally cease. Your life energy will be freed from the slavery of condemnation and opened to the fulfillment of your life purpose.

Self forgiveness is what Love wants for you. Forgiveness honors your life. Do you want your best friends to forgive themselves for mistakes they have made? Of course.

So choose to be your own best friend. Come to your own aid as a Love Master and forgive yourself generously every day.

Love Skills Quiz

I forgive myself, knowing I am learning & growing & becoming a more enlightened person...

1	2	3	4	5	6	7	8	9	10
Never		Seldom		Sometimes			Often		Always

Greeting

Others

With

Love

*The
Sacred question
of a Love Master
is not
"How loving am I?"
but
"How loved do you feel
in my presence?"*

#12

Set A

Love Intention

Greetings of love take place

in our hearts even before we meet

Love greetings begin even before you encounter another person.

For example, how are you planning to greet your love mate, closest friends, or family members the next time you see them? How are you planning to greet your co-workers today? Do you have a love intention for how you'd like to greet strangers (or might they be new friends) today?

Without thinking of your love intentions, you are likely to greet those you love with a routine greeting that does not convey the full extent of your love. Without a clear intention, you are likely to greet co-workers with your mind engaged elsewhere. And you are likely to ignore strangers and miss valuable opportunities to create more love for yourself, for others, and for the planet.

Setting love intentions is a love skill that flows through a Love Master's heart. You are fully aware of the love potential in each and every greeting. You know intuitively, even before you see someone, how deep another's need is to feel loved – even though that need may be hidden.

It only takes one party – and that would be you – to initiate a great love greeting. If the recipients of your greeting don't respond at the same level of love as you, so be it. You have created a love opening. And if they do respond, you will find yourself resonating at a deeper level of love satisfaction – all because your intention set love in motion.

By setting a love intention to greet others well, your actions move naturally towards the intention. Intentions focus your love energy into tangible reality.

On a scale of 1 to 10, how loved do you want your spouse or love mate to feel the next time you meet – even if you have already seen each other five times today? How loved do you want your kids, co-workers, or friends to feel? Do strangers today have a place of love in your life?

Thinking this way causes you to become more loving, even within your own heart, because you awake to the greater possibilities of love that exist even before a greeting takes place.

There are so many people in our world silently suffering right now – from low self-esteem, abuse, or fear of being visible. Whether this suffering is known to you or not, your intention to greet these people with healing love may be your highest contribution to the universe today.

Going forward in life with clear love intentions for each new greeting brings joy to others and to yourself. By setting love intentions, your heart is already experiencing love – even before the greeting – because you are thinking as Love. And you are ready to love.

Suppose we passed you on the street today, but you didn't recognize us. Would we feel your love? Would you feel ours? These are key questions in the heart of a Love Master.

Love Skills Quiz

I set a clear love intention before
I greet someone...

1	2	3	4	5	6	7	8	9	10
Never		Seldom		Sometimes			Often		Always

13
Smile
with Love

An open, generous, & loving smile

melts hearts

Whenever you let loose your beautiful, unrestrained smile with a heart full of love and soft eye contact, other hearts will melt in your presence.

It feels absolutely wonderful to receive the gift of someone's open, genuine smile – even if it's a stranger. Through your smile, you feel connected at a soul level. Hearts connect. You feel refreshed. Something within you comes alive.

When you smile, the love in your heart becomes visible. The genuineness and warmth of your smile gives an assurance that all is well. One smile wipes out a world of loneliness, doubt, and fear.

Smiling does wonders for your own heart too. It brings happiness out of hiding. It causes the rich, highest you to become visible – even to yourself.

So why don't we smile more? What would cause you to withhold the gift of your smile? Be aware today of anything that would talk you out of giving your smile. Consider the following story.

We have a large, close-up portrait of an elderly woman from Turkmenistan hanging in our living room. Her smile lights up our entire house. This beautiful, framed photo of her wide-open smile has been in our home, radiating love for more than 10 years. By world standards, she wouldn't be considered beautiful. She is older, over weight, and even somewhat toothless.

Yet, her heart says it all! Scott took this candid shot on a tour of Central Asia. Little did this woman realize what her whole-hearted smile would mean to us. Her smile brings joy to our hearts every single day.

That's the power of your smile too.

As you become more aware of the awesome power of your smile to bring joy and upliftment to others, this awareness brings greater sensitivity to the possibilities of this moment. What strangers will you encounter today in your life who need to feel your smile? What close friends are in need of the warm, loving assurance of your smile?

Practice being a Love Master today with your smile. Look for opportunities to say "I love you" to strangers just with your passing smile.

Pause now and connect with your inner heart. Allow it to unfold outwardly as a smile. Let your heart smile go out to the whole world. Keep smiling from your heart during this brief moment, until you know you have left your love imprint on everyone. Let your smile include everyone, even those you don't particularly like.

This is what it feels like to think and live as a Love Master.

There is nothing sweeter about you than your open, beautiful, generous, and healing smile!

The entire world says "Thank you!"

Love Skills Quiz

When greeting others,
I smile openly, generously, & genuinely...

1	2	3	4	5	6	7	8	9	10
Never		Seldom		Sometimes			Often		Always

#14

Connect

with Your Eyes

When your eyes connect & hold the space of

intimacy for even a few seconds,

you create love

Direct, soft eye contact is an uncomfortable love skill for many people to learn. We are accustomed to greetings with very little eye contact. Even in our intimate relationships, we can feel uncomfortable with sustained eye contact.

But sustained, loving eye contact connects you to love and creates immediate intimacy.

Direct, soft eye contact says to the other person, "You are special to me and nothing is more important in this moment than our genuine heart connection."

Imagine if everyone who greeted you today smiled generously at you and held steady eye contact with you for a few seconds.

Some recipients of sustained eye contact, even when it is soft and loving, may shy away. It may feel like an interruption to their isolation. Yet even in their discomfort, they will feel your love as something special and warming. They may be yearning inside to be more at ease with such intimacy.

Your sensitivity as a Love Master knows this and gives

them the perfect amount of eye contact – being sensitive to their comfort level.

Others will welcome your soft, direct eye contact, especially as it arrives simultaneously with a smile pouring generously from your heart. Such reciprocal eye connection is more powerful than words and creates a special, suspended moment of love.

Here too is where the first love skill, Love alignment, comes back into play as a valuable skill of a Love Master. Rather than feeling awkward looking into someone's eyes, especially if they are uneasy, think of yourself as Love itself looking into their eyes.

Love is thinking, "I want this person to feel pure love in this lovely moment of life."

There is only you and Love. You and Love are one. Awkwardness surrenders in this Love alignment and the receiver of your Love-directed eye contact will feel the shift.

A Love Master knows that soft, direct eye contact is an immediate path to intimacy – and wants to share this with everyone in the universe.

You are this presence of Love each time you let Love use your eyes and smile to say, "I love you" to another, even a stranger.

This is the joy in a Love Master's heart. There are no strangers in Love – so it is natural for our eyes to connect and say hello with love.

Love Skills Quiz

When greeting others, I look directly, but softly, into their eyes & hold this contact for a few seconds...

1	2	3	4	5	6	7	8	9	10
Never		Seldom		Sometimes			Often		Always

#15

Hug
with Empathy

A perfect hug greets others
with an open, flowing heart but also
a keen sensitivity to their needs

A good hug can instantly create a warm, intimate feeling of heart-to-heart connection. Hugs can feel absolutely wonderful!

But hugs are a sensitive thing. Some people love to hug. Others don't.

So what is a "good" hug?

When you are about to hug someone as a Love Master, quickly peek into the other's heart with your intuition. Is their heart open and welcoming your hug? Is their heart already retreating for safety in the greeting? Or are they in the middle zone where you're not quite sure?

This pre moment of love is the beginning of loving them with a sensitive heart – even before a word has been spoken.

It's a joy, of course, when two open hearts greet each other. The hug flows out naturally and with easy giving and receiving. It feels wonderful to both parties.

When you sense that someone doesn't want to hug, however, you can go for a loving hand shake but also convey your love with a radiant smile and direct, soft eye contact.

If someone is in the middle ground on hugs and you're not sure what to do, this is a wonderful moment to create love safety. You might ask them if they'd like a hug. Or give them a more polite hug that doesn't infringe on their boundaries.

Give yourself permission to experiment with your hugging love skill. And pay attention to the refinements of a good hug.

Some people hug like two ironing boards greeting each other – stiff & straight with no flexibility or flow.

Others give the "football hug" with one shoulder leaning into you, like they are defending themselves or making sure this hug isn't going to get too personal.

Others hug with the "A-frame hug." They bend way forward so there is only the slightest coming together of bodies at the top end. Safe, but not much love juice.

It is understandable that some people are defensive in receiving hugs. Many women have experienced some men's hugs as too intimate or as sexual advances. And we've all suffered from "bear hugs" where we almost cringe in pain or gasp for air – and freedom.

A Love Master is aware of these issues before he or she gives a hug – and as a hug is being given.

A perfect hug is close, genuine, and intimate, but not too close or crossing the line. And it ends just when the other wants it to end. A perfect hug may last for two seconds with one person and ten seconds with another.

Explore using your hug as a way of creating more love with the deeply caring sensitivity of a Love Master.

Love Skills Quiz

When greeting others, I hug them with an open heart but also with a keen sensitivity to their needs...

1	2	3	4	5	6	7	8	9	10
Never		Seldom		Sometimes			Often		Always

#16

Voice

A Love Message

Voicing a love message

sets a tone of goodwill & causes someone

to feel acknowledged & appreciated

Greetings are often short – just a few seconds. Yet your clear love intention, open smile, and loving eyes can convey an enormous amount of love in a brief moment.

A short love message is like icing on your greeting cake. So what is a love message?

A good love message is a very short heart statement of how you feel right there in the moment of the greeting. A love message tells someone that she or he is special. For example, with someone you already know and appreciate, you might convey your love like this:

- "It's a delight to see you again."
- "It always feels good to be with you."
- "I'm so grateful you are in my life."
- "Every time I see you, my heart feels good."
- "I so admire what you are contributing with your life."

With someone you are meeting for the first time, you might convey a genuine love message in a different way:

- "I love your smile. It radiates joy."

- "Your eyes are so beautiful and full of love."
- "I'm very delighted to meet you."
- "I look forward to knowing you."

You would only voice such love messages, of course, if you genuinely felt these thoughts. If you're a bit stuck at finding something to say, look more closely so you can discover and appreciate someone's smile, eyes, or something else special – perhaps even something they are wearing.

All these love messages have one thing in common. They voice your love in a genuine way to another's heart.

Whether or not you have time for a greeting to develop into a longer conversation or greater intimacy, you have created an authentic love moment that will last for a long time in the other person's heart – and in yours.

"I don't think I can be that bold," you might be thinking. It's actually not about boldness. It's about choosing to live your life in the arena of intimacy and love rather than live in separation and distance.

It gets easy and fun as you practice. Start with your friends. Find new ways to greet them with a love message. Notice how they feel, even though they know you love them (perhaps they're not so sure). Don't worry about finding the right words. Let your heart create the words. Love has an infinite number of ways to say "I love you."

By voicing a love message, you make a deeply satisfying connection every time you greet someone. Your love message sets a tone of goodwill and causes the other person to feel acknowledged and appreciated.

Love Skills Quiz

When greeting someone, I voice a short
but genuine love message so he or she will feel loved...

1	2	3	4	5	6	7	8	9	10
Never		Seldom		Sometimes			Often		Always

Creating

Intimacy

*Creating intimacy
opens hearts
to
immediate
love fulfillment*

#17

Decide to Create Intimacy

A Love Master is proactive

& takes the lead in creating intimacy

Genuine intimacy is the key to love fulfillment. Intimacy causes our hearts to feel connected and not alone. We taste the sweetness of genuine love.

Real intimacy occurs whenever you relate to someone from the heart. When you wear a mask socially and act superficially, this is the opposite of genuine intimacy.

When two hearts open and communicate, something astonishing and wonderful happens. There is inner relief to be "real." There is also immense discovery and deeper appreciation for each other.

This is the quality of relationship you can have with just about anybody – if you want to.

That brings you face-to-face with a key life decision. Do you want heart connections? Do you want to know what truly makes someone tick at the heart level? Do you want to be real and unmasked in your relationships? Do you want to live a heart-centered life of communication?

Think of the very best relationships you have in your life. What makes them valuable and rich?

Our best relationships include compassion, open hearts, shared feelings, humor, and little or no judgment. We feel emotionally safe.

Unfortunately, genuine intimacy is rare and not the norm in most people's lives. We wait to let the other party make the first move to share from the heart. Our relationships are often reactive rather than proactive.

Rather than waiting to see what someone else is going to do, a Love Master makes the decision to create intimacy. Just making this decision opens the door to intimacy because others will feel your intention.

Can you have genuine intimacy with everyone you meet? Just about. You'll be surprised how open others are to a genuine heart connection when you take the initiative as a Love Master.

Intimacy is really your choice. It doesn't even matter whether the other party responds. You, as a Love Master, have created the opportunity for more love. You will feel better about yourself no matter what happens.

The moment to create intimacy presents itself many times each day – with family members, friends, co-workers, grocery clerks, and those you meet moving through life.

How much love do you really want in your life? How loved do you want others to feel in your presence? Without being proactive in creating love, you are likely to have superficial, polite conversations from the head rather than genuine friendships and intimacy from the heart.

Once you decide to create intimacy, the rest becomes quite easy.

Welcome to the consciousness of a Love Master and a whole new world of love fulfillment.

Love Skills Quiz

I am proactive & take the lead in creating genuine intimacy when I am with someone...

1	2	3	4	5	6	7	8	9	10
Never		Seldom		Sometimes			Often		Always

#18

Be Present &
Tune in as Love

When you are present & tuned in,
you are focused on love & its vast potential
in this very moment

When your sweet love greeting has finished, you quickly arrive at a new threshold of love opportunity.

Right here in this flicker of a moment, you have the choice to be present and tune in as Love – or let this opportunity for intimacy slip away.

When you are present and tuned in, you are focusing on love and its vast potential in this very moment. You are not distracted by other people, events, circumstances, or thinking about something else. In this state of love readiness, you carry within you all the rich possibilities of love, so alive and real to you.

You check in with yourself. Am I in Love alignment? Allow Love to flood into your being so you are not feeling awkward or questioning whether you have the capability. Love has the skill.

Let your heart tune in to this person and ask: "What does my intuition tell me is going on and needed with this unique individual in front of me right now? In your intuition scan, ask yourself, "Does this person need...

- Comfort?
- Encouragement?
- Acknowledgment of worth?
- Praise?
- Support for facing a problem?
- An opportunity to speak and be heard?
- Or just a chance to be playful?"

As you listen to Love for the answer to your intuition, you will be amazed at how clearly you will sense the many love options open to you. There is no one right option. Love has a multitude of excellent possibilities in each moment of intimacy.

In some cases, you might be guided to give the person a huge embrace from Love because you sense so clearly that this is needed and welcome. In other cases you may be led to listen as you sense a need to talk. Or you may feel it's best for you to initiate talk from the heart.

You may be guided just to continue staying present with your smile and eyes. This alone can take any greeting past the doorway of love and into genuine intimacy and dialogue.

In some cases, you may not get a solid reading from your intuition. This is a wonderful opportunity to ask a love question, one of the most magnificent love skills for creating genuine intimacy.

What is a love question?

We thought you'd never ask.

Please turn the page to the next love skill, "Ask a Love Question."

Love Skills Quiz

When I am with someone, I am present & tuned in, focusing on the vast potential of love in the moment...

1	2	3	4	5	6	7	8	9	10
Never		Seldom		Sometimes			Often		Always

#19

Ask a

Love Question

Asking a "Love Question"

is one of the most powerful love skills

for creating genuine intimacy

Love questions open hearts in amazing ways. This is one of the biggest of all the love skills.

So, what is a "love question?"

Here are some examples that open wide the doors to intimacy when you are with someone. You can ask:

- "What are you most passionate about?"
- "What is the most significant thing going on in your life?"
- "What's the best thing going on in your life?"
- "What's going on in your heart?"
- "What are you thinking?"
- "What is calling you higher in your life?
- "What do you feel is your highest life purpose?"

These are questions that speak directly to another's heart. You will be surprised at how easily most people will answer them – openly and genuinely. You will find yourself experiencing genuine intimacy immediately – and all because you took the initiative to ask a simple, but profound love question.

For greatest success with a love question, set the stage so the other person sees that something different is about to occur. Looking into the other's eyes with a smile and a genuine heart, you might say, "I'd like to ask you a question." Let them feel something special is happening.

Sometimes, when you ask a love question, there will be a pause – even a long pause. That's because these are big questions and may catch another's heart by surprise – but delightfully. Give them silence to think about the wonderful question.

It's not unusual for someone to quietly question your authenticity by looking deep into your soul and wondering, "Do you really want to know?" "Are you being genuine in asking me this question?" "Are you for real?" You can assure them you are with your smile and attitude.

Love questions are the mark of the presence of a Love Master. You know there may be awkwardness, but you know that a love question opens a relationship to immediate intimacy. Rather than feeling awkward or wondering if you'll look stupid or be rejected, your heart flows back to love skill #1 – Love alignment.

Let Love ask the question and choose the words. Let Love use you as the vehicle. Let your ego disappear and enjoy the love adventure. You don't need to know the outcome in advance. The process creates intimacy.

There is great joy in asking a love question. It says to another person "You are special." It also calls forth your own highest love self. Love questions flow from the internal, sacred question of a Love Master, "How loved do you feel in my presence?"

Love Skills Quiz

When I am with someone, I ask "love questions" such as "What are you most passionate about?...

1	2	3	4	5	6	7	8	9	10
Never		Seldom		Sometimes			Often		Always

#20

Listen

with Empathy

Empathy is the most

profound and convincing way to say

"I love you!"

Empathy is a rare skill on Earth – so far. That will change, however, as people discover the immense love riches that pour forth from listening to others with empathy.

Empathy is the love skill of tuning in to another person with so much sensitivity that you can sense what the other person is feeling and understand what the other person is saying with great accuracy. Yet you remain independent at the same time.

Sympathy with another person causes you to become lodged, even trapped in their "story" and feelings. Empathy, on the other hand, means that you can put yourself in another's shoes and sense how he or she feels. Empathy causes you to know and love another at the deepest level of compassion yet still maintain your own detachment and freedom.

Empathy is perhaps the #1 tool of counselors and therapists because they know your heart needs to be heard and understood. When someone's heart is genuinely heard, he or she feels relief, understanding, care, and love.

Do you know anyone whose heart needs to be heard

and understood? On a scale of 1 to 10, to what extent do your spouse, children, best friends, co-workers, and everyone else you know, feel they are truly heard and understood by you?"

For many of these people, the answer to this question may be low. Why? Because when people sense that you are not genuinely tuned in, they stop sharing from their heart. Hearts need an invitation of real love to share openly. You may not even realize that you are the catalyst for their shut down.

Here's the good news. Listening with empathy is not a difficult love skill to learn. Most people are just not accustomed to doing it – or have never been taught how.

Here's how to practice and refine the skill of listening with empathy.

When someone begins to talk, hit the mute button on your internal self talk and let your entire focus be acutely tuned to hearing what the other person is saying. Stay silent. This is their moment. Allow yourself to deeply hear, feel, and understand what they are saying or feeling. Don't worry about the details. Just keep listening with keen awareness and no distractions. The other person will feel the depth of your caring without you even saying a word. You deserve to receive this quality of love as well.

The advantages of empathy are like discovering a love gold mine. Other's hearts feel safe, heard, understood, and deeply loved by you. You discover all sorts of new and valuable things about others.

Listening with empathy creates deep intimacy and is one of the top love skills of a Love Master.

Love Skills Quiz

When someone is speaking from the heart,
I listen with empathy...

1	2	3	4	5	6	7	8	9	10
Never		Seldom		Sometimes			Often		Always

#21

Accept
without Judgment

*Acceptance without judgment
is an invisible love skill that creates intimacy,
freedom, & massive goodwill*

Acceptance without judgment is another rare but profound love skill.

How many people in your life accept you without judgment?

For most of us, the answer might be no one, one person, or just a handful. In other words, not many.

How many people in your life feel accepted without judgment by you? The answer to this might be revealing.

Most of us were simply never taught or have never experienced this empowering love skill.

For a Love Master, acceptance without judgment is an often invisible love skill that creates intimacy, freedom, and massive goodwill. Other's hearts feel totally cherished by acceptance without judgment. An environment of acceptance causes their hearts to open like flowers feeling the warmth of sunshine.

Here's how to practice the love skill of accepting others without judgment. It may not be easy at first, but every practice of this skill will demonstrate its value and will strengthen you as a Love Master.

When you are with others, make a conscious decision to accept them without judgment. Suspend all judgment of "right" or "wrong," "good" or "bad," "wise" or "stupid."

Instead, just love them as they are. Let go of all scoring of what they are saying and doing. Just enjoy them. Let them feel your acceptance of them as worthy, intelligent, and lovable.

You don't have to agree with what they are doing or saying. Let go of the role of being a mental police officer, advisor, or authority. Relax and accept.

You will be quite surprised at the outcome of acceptance without judgment. Others will feel your attitude of genuine love even though it's invisible. They will begin to feel safe. They will open their hearts. They will explore ideas with more freedom. They will come to new conclusions in the safety of your non-judgmental, loving environment. They will feel deeply loved.

You may be surprised at what happens within you. As you genuinely accept others without judgment, you will see the power of your genuine acceptance washing through them. You will feel good about yourself. You will feel what it feels like to be a Love Master in action.

Acceptance without judgment is a highly refined love skill because it takes enormous patience, restraint, and practice.

The love payoffs, however, are off the charts.

Love Skills Quiz

I accept others without judgment...

1	2	3	4	5	6	7	8	9	10
Never		Seldom		Sometimes			Often		Always

#22

Use Silence as a Love Tool

When a heart that is speaking

encounters your loving silence,

it opens even wider

Listening with silence is a profound way of honoring another's heart.

The temptation, of course, is to interrupt and respond to someone sharing because you too have lots to say. Or perhaps what has been said has triggered a response within you. It's often not easy to be silent.

By choosing to remain silent, despite this triggering, you let the ball stay in the other person's court. He or she remains in control of where the conversation next moves. Relax, knowing you will have a turn soon enough.

Silence creates freedom for the other person speaking. He or she can even take time to pause and reflect before sharing more, because your loving silence says, without words, "This is your moment to let your heart fully speak. I want to honor you and give you maximum freedom to explore and share."

You are practicing great listening! Let your body language also show your interest – by eye contact, active facial interest, and even leaning closer at times.

We all know what it feels like when we are sharing from

the heart and another person just can't wait to speak. We feel the interrupting pressure, even if it is unstated. So we usually close down our hearts, stop speaking, and come to a close. Our intimacy level drops dramatically. And they might not have a clue why.

Whenever another person is speaking deeply from the heart, or you want to encourage someone to be open at a deeper level, silence is a golden love skill.

When using the love skill of silence, there may be awkward moments. Even a few seconds of silence can seem so empty that you might feel compelled to say something.

Yet right here in this void or empty space is a place where deep insight, love, healing, and intimacy can thrive. In silence, others become assured of your genuine interest. It's so rare, however, that they may feel a bit stunned. Remember that silence is not a negative void but a quiet, restful place of reflection. Be comfortable with your silence. Feel its loving power. Let it work its wonders.

As you become skilled in being silent, you will discover that others begin sharing at a new level of intimacy. They may use a few seconds of the silence to test the sincerity of your heart before they open even more. But in genuine silence, their hearts will open.

Silence is another invisible love skill. When someone is silent and gives our heart space to express itself in freedom and safety, we feel genuinely loved even though we may not know why or how this happened.

Silence is a treasured secret of a Love Master.

Love Skills Quiz

When I am listening, I use silence
as a tool of love...

1	2	3	4	5	6	7	8	9	10
Never		Seldom		Sometimes			Often		Always

#23

"Tell Me More..."

Three little love words

"Tell me more..."

create entire new worlds of intimacy

"Tell me more..." When these three little words are softly stated while you are listening to someone, he or she will feel immensely loved and will continue sharing at an even richer level of soul.

Your goal as a Love Master is to fully hear and understand another person's heart and also to create an environment where this person can fully hear his or her own heart. These are empowering and enriching love motives.

It is more normal in our lives, however, to almost compete for a turn in a conversation. Often we just give up trying. So when we speak and then a Love Master says to us, "Tell me more..." we may be stunned. We might even think, "Could this be true? Does this person genuinely want to know more from me?"

And then an internal question might also surface within us in the silence, "What more do I actually have to say? I need time to reflect on this before speaking. But oh, this silence and respect and honoring feel so good. I feel genuinely loved. Let me see, what do I want to say now that I feel safer and more genuinely loved?"

That's the internal dialogue that is often going on within another when you combine silence with the encouraging phrase, "Tell me more..."

Do you see the enormous love impact these three little words can have when combined with genuine and encouraging silence?

You can repeat these three little words often. You might find new ways to say the same thing, but the beauty of "Tell me more..." is that it leaves it entirely up to the other party to decide what to talk about.

For example, suppose you said: "You just mentioned your sister. Tell me more about your sister?" This might seem very loving and, actually it is loving. But it also forces the person to now talk more about the sister. You, not the other person, have now set the agenda. Without knowing it, you may have derailed an opportunity for even deeper intimacy.

If you had simply said, "Tell me more..." the other person might have talked about the sister or might have found his or her heart moving in an entirely new direction, basking in the freedom of your love space. Let the other person be the decision-maker.

"Tell me more..." is another almost invisible love skill. It ever so gently keeps a conversation moving and expanding but in a completely unobtrusive way.

You'll be happier too, in your own relationships, when you make space for your friends to ask you those golden words "Tell me more...."

By the way, we have a love question for you: What's going on in *your* heart right now?

Tell me more...

Love Skills Quiz

When listening & someone finishes a thought & pauses, I encouragingly say, "Tell me more..."

1	2	3	4	5	6	7	8	9	10
Never		Seldom		Sometimes			Often		Always

#24

Reflect Back & Validate

To truly hear & understand another being

is one of the highest gifts of love

you can give

Listening is a wonderful love skill. But how do others know you have actually heard them? In fact, how do *you* know you have accurately heard them?

The beauty of reflecting back and validating is that you can confirm that you have accurately heard what has been said.

Here's how it is done.

When listening to someone, he or she will eventually come to a place of true ending, where the love skills of silence or "Tell me more..." are no longer needed.

This end point is the perfect moment to reflect back what you think you heard. Try to summarize in your own words what you heard. Don't judge what has been said or give your interpretation. Just state what you think you heard. A successful way to do this is to start by saying, "What I hear you saying is..." and then add at the end, "Is that accurate?"

Be silent. Let them respond. They may pause. Don't think this is about you being judged. It's still about the other person. Was this person heard and understood?

That's the key question in your heart.

If your reflecting back is accurate, the person will say or indicate "Yes" and often keep on talking – at an even deeper level of openness and intimacy.

If your empathy was off, the person will say so and (if your love is still present and active in your heart) you will get another chance to listen with more keenness. Remember, this is not about you. This is about the other person. Did you hear accurately? Your heart wants to know. If you were off, you want to get it right.

Why? Because to truly hear and understand another being is one of the highest gifts of love you can give. As a Love Master, you want genuine intimacy and you know the loving power of reflecting back and validating what another has shared.

Reflecting back is a subtle love skill. To do it well, you don't merely repeat another's words. You state what you heard in your own words, but without judging or changing the meaning. This is one of the keys to the art of loving.

You can also reflect back on a feeling level. Even though you may have heard lots of words, your reflecting back might be, "What I hear you feeling is that you are a bit worried about this transition but confident at the same time. Is that accurate?"

And the response back to you might be, "Well, almost. I'd say..." and the person will clarify in more detail. The result will be genuine love and expanded intimacy.

Reflecting back and validating is a top love skill in the tool kit of a Love Master.

Love Skills Quiz

After listening, I reflect back what I have heard in order to validate the accuracy of my listening...

1	2	3	4	5	6	7	8	9	10
Never		Seldom		Sometimes			Often		Always

#25

Honor Soul

When you honor another's soul,

your heart is saying

"I admire & love your Highest Self"

Imagine how you feel after sharing openly from your heart to another person.

You may feel a bit vulnerable. Am I still liked? Is what I said important? Am I worthy? These are natural internal feelings within a heart that has revealed itself openly as a result of someone's empathetic listening, silence, and encouraging "Tell me more..."

This is precisely the moment to openly honor another's soul – someone's Highest Self. Share openly how much you admire this person. How special he or she is. Or how much you appreciate what has been shared with you.

Honoring someone's soul means that you pronounce aloud how wonderful this person is and how valuable you find what has been shared. This is a wonderful opportunity to share insights into their core self.

Don't hold back. Find the words that reveal and clarify how much you honor other's ideas. Or the importance of a person's life. Or their value to you. Don't be skimpy. Be generous with your words and love.

When you honor another's soul, the recipient of your honoring feels a wave of relief and joy and love flow through his or her entire psyche. It feels so wonderful to be honored for who we are – to be truly seen as valuable!

How many people in your life honor your soul openly and profusely?

For most of us, the sad answer is, "Not many."

That's why honoring another's soul is one of the refined secrets of a Love Master and such an important love skill. As a Love Master, you know – without it needing to be said – how important it is for someone to feel worthy and for their worth to be validated openly with your words.

For example, we'd like to honor *your* soul right now and say to you, "There is something we really value about you – even though we may have never met. We admire your deep commitment to growing in love and your desire to live as a Love Master. That says so much about your character and your heart. We applaud who you are!"

It is pure joy to honor another's soul. It is like giving a priceless gift to another being. What is more meaningful than confirmation of the rich value of our lives?

Be ready and eager to honor soul with everyone you meet. Go past focusing on looks and lifestyle to honoring what you see unfolding in the depth of their being. Your love energy will be felt and appreciated.

As you practice this skill of honoring soul with everyone you encounter, you will find yourself operating and living at a level of soul awareness that honors your own soul and Highest Self.

As you scan your life and the people you know and see everyday, and the new people you will encounter today, how many of them need their soul to be known and loved by you?

As a Love Master, you think this way.

And act.

Love Skills Quiz

After listening to someone, I tell him or her how special and valuable he or she is...

1	2	3	4	5	6	7	8	9	10
Never		Seldom		Sometimes			Often		Always

#26

Be

Transparent

Transparency allows hearts
to share openly
& connect

Being transparent causes hearts to move rapidly into openness and genuine intimacy.

Whenever you speak to someone with an open heart and a willingness to reveal your true self, you are being transparent. You allow others to see into your thinking, heart, and soul without barriers, role-playing, or emotional games. You let down your walls.

It is a joy to be with someone who is transparent. Hearts feel refreshed and open. We feel like we are receiving an invitation to genuine intimacy. Communication is real!

The beauty of transparency is that, whenever you take the plunge to being transparent yourself, others in your presence will find their hearts opening as well – uncontrollably!

A Love Master is keenly aware of the power of transparency to create genuine intimacy and strives to live with a heart that is ready and willing to be an open window with others.

Such openness may seem to make you vulnerable, but it actually causes you to become more at ease with your core self – the real, magnificent you alive and visible at last.

As you practice transparency, others will feel more emotionally safe and open with their hearts as well.

They will also feel more loved because you are being emotionally honest and real with them. They will appreciate you more because they are seeing the genuine, real you – which is always more lovable than the pretend, disguised, or hiding you.

Being transparent does not mean you have to spill your guts and openly reveal every single challenge you are facing in your life with everyone you meet.

As a Love Master, you adapt easily to various levels of openness in relationships. Some relationships allow you to be fully transparent because you know you are loved and safe. Others may feel more restrictive. As a Love Master, you learn to sense when transparency can be a valuable way to create intimacy.

Rather than thinking that being transparent is a risk, you understand the intimacy payoffs of revealing your true self and choosing to be with others who do the same.

If someone doesn't respond to your heart, this may not be a relationship that will serve you at the level of soul. Let your heart move on. As a Love Master practicing transparency, you have bravely taken the initiative to create a maximum love opportunity. This is all that Love wants you to do. Be unattached to the outcomes.

Transparency takes relationships to a higher level of soul satisfaction and is a top love skill of a Love Master

---

Love Skills Quiz

I am transparent (open) when I am
communicating with others...

1	2	3	4	5	6	7	8	9	10
Never		Seldom		Sometimes			Often		Always

#27

Speak with Gentleness

Speaking with gentleness

soothes hearts

& allows intimacy to flow

Creating intimacy is all about the process – *how* you speak rather than what you say. When you speak with gentleness, intimacy flourishes. When gentleness is absent, intimacy disappears.

Gentleness is easy to overlook when you are in a hurry to discuss what you want to say. Your words may be accurate, but they may be so direct or blunt that they create unease or even conflict. Intimacy easily slips away without gentleness.

Rather than waiting until intimacy erodes or evolves into conflict and then hitting your "speak with gentleness" button, use this love skill to create a smooth path of sustained and flowing intimacy.

As a Love Master, constantly think about *how* to say something in a way that enhances intimacy rather than just focusing on getting your point across.

Here is an example. Suppose you are talking with someone and intimacy between you is flowing nicely. Then, however, something is said that you disagree with. Which words below would flow from you and what would be the effect of your choice?

A. "I disagree with what you are saying."

B. "I'm enjoying our conversation and I respect what you are saying. I have a slightly different point of view on this issue and I'd like to share that for conversation."

The first example is direct. You may be correct, but these words don't create or sustain intimacy. In fact, intimacy would most likely decline or even disappear after this one statement.

With the second example, you still get your point across, but with a gentle smoothness that also allows intimacy to continue to flow. The difference in the two responses is vast.

Do you see the power of this love skill?

To be an expert in speaking with gentleness, stay connected to the *process*. Think *how*, not what. Choose your words with care. Think with your heart as well as your head. Use words that unite rather than divide.

Let your tone be soft and loving rather than pushing or adamant. Take time to be attuned to how the other person is receiving your words. There is no need to rush. Keep your focus on sustaining intimacy.

Speaking with gentleness calms and soothes everyone's heart. It allows intimacy to flow as a steady wave with hardly a ripple. It is not only polite, but noble.

A Love Master continually expresses gentleness as a refined consideration of another's heart.

Love Skills Quiz

I speak with gentleness to soothe hearts & allow intimacy to flow...

1	2	3	4	5	6	7	8	9	10
Never		Seldom		Sometimes			Often		Always

#28

Share from Your Own Heart

Speaking up
& sharing from your heart
honors your own worth

Intimacy honors all parties. Each heart needs to be listened to and heard. This includes your heart.

In the real world, some people may not ask about you. They may not know how to check in with your heart. They may not have any idea how to create love equality. They may not yet have learned the love skills in this book.

As a Love Master, you have compassion for this love oversight and realize that any inquiry about you may never happen.

What then? How will you share what they don't even know how to solicit? How will your treasure of expression and essence be known?

This calls for love leadership. You can be an equality instigator by saying, "Thank you for sharing your heart so openly. I'd like to share what's going on in my heart too."

You are making the assumption they want to know. And you will soon find out if they do. Those untrained in love skills may intend or wish to get around to listening to you, but they just don't. So you are taking the lead by taking your turn and sharing from your own heart.

Another way to ensure your heart gets heard is to set it up in advance. For example, you might say, "I'm so glad we are having lunch together. Let's take turns sharing what's in each of our hearts. Why don't you take the first few minutes and I'll go next."

This creates equality from the start line. But you, as an aware Love Master, may still have to ensure that your turn actually comes. You might even have to break in after a few minutes and say, "I'm glad you've shared so openly. I'd like to share what's going on with me too. Perhaps we can go back and forth." And then start sharing.

Want to be creative with this love skill? Tell them, "Would you like to know what I would like you to ask me?" Who would turn down such a fun and curious question!

Or give them a love question to ask you. Pick from the chapter on Love questions, or make up one based on what is most current and interesting to you. They may like the question so much they want to answer it too!

If you are a giving and loving person, you are very good at listening to others. But when it comes time to take a turn for yourself, you may be less skilled. If you find this a skill you need to improve, see how many times you can practice it in coming weeks. As you practice it, keep encouraging yourself with each success.

Afterwards, evaluate how you felt doing it. How could you have done it better? What was the response? How do you feel about the response? See how much there is to learn about love!

Sharing from your own heart honors you as *you* deserve to be treated as a Love Master.

Love Skills Quiz

I speak up & share from my heart to
honor my own worth....

1	2	3	4	5	6	7	8	9	10
Never		Seldom		Sometimes		Often			Always

#29

Act

with Integrity

Integrity is the foundation

for enduring & loving relationships

Integrity in relationships strengthens and sustains intimacy. Many budding relationships never get to bloom because of a breakdown in integrity.

Integrity doesn't mean that you can lie as long as you don't get caught. It means there is no hidden agenda. It means you can be trusted and your words and actions are reliable and true.

How is your integrity in relationships? Here's a quick integrity check list:

- Do you do what you say you will do?
- Do you act differently when someone is not looking or aware?
- Do you withhold or hide information – or lie?
- Are there any unmentioned relationships?
- Do you consistently keep your word?
- Are you reliably on time?

These are some of the areas where a relationship breaks down.

Living in integrity takes courage. It's easy and tempting to be dishonest. Integrity means you rise to your highest place, regardless of consequences, and you remain honest to yourself as well as others. You speak truth. Integrity is earned through the times you are tempted to act outside of integrity, but decided instead to base your life on something you can admire and respect. It takes humility to live by principles of integrity. As a Love Master, you are proud of yourself for living in integrity.

A Love Master chooses friends, lovers, and business associates based on integrity. Sometimes a Love Master uses his or her intuition since a lack of integrity often doesn't surface for awhile in relationships.

How important is integrity to you?

Integrity needs to come up as one of the first things you notice in others. Living and acting with integrity means you have far fewer stresses, losses, and disappointments. When someone is accountable, you find out where the bumps are early and can deal with them far easier than the surprise that comes later when you discover on your own that someone has been hiding truth from you. Trust is the backbone of a loving relationship.

As a Love Master living in integrity, you have deeper intimacy based on trust – even though your honesty may sometimes cause a ripple in a relationship.

Living in integrity means you act and speak based on truth, not based on what is convenient. It means you can be counted on by others. People believe what you say because you have proven your integrity. You are admired because everyone knows how difficult it is to live in integrity.

In short, you are a true Love Master, fully aware that integrity is the foundation for enduring and loving relationships.

Love Skills Quiz

I act with integrity in my relationships....

1	2	3	4	5	6	7	8	9	10
Never		Seldom		Sometimes			Often		Always

Expanding

Love

*Love
can expand
in
infinite
ways*

#30

Be

Responsive

A Love Master responds to hearts

yearning for connection

Love expands the moment we are responsive to another's heart.

When someone's heart opens and reaches out to you, – in person, by phone, or email – this is a "Love Master moment." It is a moment where you as a Love Master quickly and genuinely respond to this invitation for more love.

Have you ever made a love overture that was met with no response, or a delayed response. Our hearts wait. We assume the worst. We begin to retreat. Many love expansion opportunities are lost from lack of responsiveness.

Is someone waiting for your response right now?

Responsiveness is more challenging today because of the deluge of voice mails, text messages, and emails. There has never been such pressure to respond. Many feel overwhelmed by the necessity to respond, respond, respond! Our sensitivities are on high alert. How do we respond to everyone and instantly, all the time?

As a Love Master, you care about other's hearts. When someone singles you out to communicate with from the heart, you know it deserves a response – and you are responsive.

You find the love words, however brief, that allow love to expand. It is amazing how brief a time it takes to express genuine love. It won't take any longer by waiting, but in not being responsive, Love Master moments will pass and hearts will yearn. Others will think you don't care.

Do you see the power of response? A response means that you care enough to express love. It doesn't mean you have to comply with someone's wishes which may infringe on you. It means that you are awake and responsive to other's tender hearts. You don't ignore their desire to connect.

Responsiveness is a natural outcome of compassion. When someone makes an overture of love to you – in person, by email, or by phone – tune in to this person's heart. What does this person need? What is Love prompting you to know and do? Such responsiveness within your own heart expands love even before you take action.

What simple words could speak from your heart that would let others know they are important and that you care. When you are responsive to other's hearts, even briefly, Love expands immediately.

What if you are the one waiting, longing, and hoping for a response after you have opened your heart to someone? As a Love Master, you can lovingly ask for a response – without apology or cowering. Don't retreat. Go forward in love without expecting others to read your heart. Lovingly help them to know what is important to you. Help them win. Help them become Love Masters too.

Love Skills Quiz

I am responsive to others when they open their
hearts & invite me in...

1	2	3	4	5	6	7	8	9	10
Never		Seldom		Sometimes			Often		Always

#31

Cherish Dreams

Nothing liberates the inner core

of who we are as much as someone who

cherishes our dreams

Within each of us are vast, creative dreams. We dream of what we would like to be, do, and accomplish.

For most of us, however, these dreams lay buried within the secrets of our inner soul. Our dreams are sometimes so fragile that we are too embarrassed to reveal them – sometimes even to ourselves.

It feels frightening to reveal them to those around us. What would they think? Who are we to have such dreams? Yet these dreams persist in our private consciousness. In fact, they carry our full life potential, our destiny. That's how valuable they are!

Nothing liberates the inner core of who we are as much as someone who cherishes our dreams and loves us so deeply that our richest, core identity is brought to the surface, recognized, and gloriously valued. Genuine love helps to liberate dreams.

Each of us is like a gem at the bottom of the ocean, hidden by layers of timidity and accepted limitations. Each of us needs each other to encourage our inner flower to bloom.

An environment of genuine love, kindness, gentleness, caring, and patience allows dreams to surface. And there's more. Dreams need room to be spoken and explored. This is the environment that a Love Master seeks to create.

Once you cause another's heart to feel safe, you can ask, "What is your biggest dream for your life?"

Then use your silent, attentive listening to call it forward. Use the love skills of silence and "Tell me more..." Let this question occur in all your special relationships.

Do you know the life dreams of your loved ones and friends? If not, you can practice this love skill immediately. Since our dreams are forever evolving, you can ask this honoring question often.

What is *your* biggest dream for your own life?

As you ponder this, please know that we hold the highest and most cherished place for your dreams. There are no wrong answers. There is nothing to judge. Take your time. This is an important question. Deep within, your heart's message wants to be known, appreciated, and valued. Your dream reveals the real inner you and it is gorgeous – we promise! We already love your dreams!

As greater clarity comes forward, ask yourself, "If I took one action towards my top dream, what would it be?"

Give yourself plenty of quiet, meditative time to reflect on this important question. It often helps to journal. Please continue listening to the voice within – the one with the dream of your destiny. As you do so, what now seems to be a far away dream will become a living reality in your life.

This is how a Love Master cherishes dreams.

Love Skills Quiz

I take my relationships higher by cherishing others' dreams as well as my own...

1	2	3	4	5	6	7	8	9	10
Never		Seldom		Sometimes			Often		Always

#32

Ask Deeper Love Questions

Deep love questions take relationships to the level of soul sharing

Y ou've already learned the power of Love questions to create intimacy.

Now it's time to learn how to ask even deeper love questions that expand love to the level of soul sharing.

Your relationships may already be good. But what would take them even higher? What would cause your relationships to soar in soul where hearts unite in bliss?

You guessed it. Deeper love questions.

For example, imagine the soul-inspiring outcomes of asking one of these questions:

- What is going on deep in your heart that might be helpful or healing for you to share?
- What are the biggest life lessons you are learning at this time in your life?
- What is the biggest challenge to happiness in your heart and soul and how are you tackling it?
- What are you not talking about because no one is asking?

- How can I best support you?
- "On a scale of 1 to 10, how loved do you feel today?"

And then ask the potent, revealing follow-up question:

- "What would make that a 10?"

These questions show that you care about someone at a deep heart level. Just asking such a question takes a relationship higher because others feel the depth of your genuine caring and love.

You will discover how quickly a relationship can transcend the ordinary and leap into soul because you took this love leadership role and asked a deeper love question.

As a Love Master, you know the delicious taste of communicating at a level of soul. It's not just an increase in love. It's a quantum leap into a love space that most people never experience.

This extraordinary love space is just a question away. Move past any barriers of awkwardness and concern and develop expertise with these questions. Invent your own soul questions. Play with them. Observe carefully how others respond. Become an expert at creating love at the soul level.

Ask these questions often. This is an excellent way to become a great listener and to empower others.

By the way, we have a deeper love question for you.

"How is your heart changing the most as a result of reading this book?"

Love Skills Quiz

To take relationships higher, I ask even deeper love questions, such as "How loved do you feel today?"...

1	2	3	4	5	6	7	8	9	10
Never		Seldom		Sometimes			Often		Always

#33

Create Unity

With every

thought, word, & action

you create unity or separation

You have amazing power to create unity in every moment in your relationships.

Moment by moment, your relationships either sink lower or rise higher based on what is in your heart and what you say and do.

As a Love Master, your heart is in such a clear state of caring for others, as well as humanity, that you consciously seek to create a stream of continuous unity.

For example, even when you are upset, you inwardly sense the potential to create unity rather than division in your relationships. You quickly seek to find greater peace in your heart so your words will flow from the dictionary of loving speech rather than the dictionary of polarization.

This may not be easy when your temperature is rising in a relationship, but it takes an incredibly long time to overcome unkind words that separate hearts. Sometimes, hearts don't ever recover. Harmony, peace, and stability of love depend on unity.

Think of creating unity as a love skill you want to master. Your goal is to quietly assess each new moment in your relationships. Rank yourself, from 1 to 10, on how well you use words and actions that create unity rather than separation. Your awareness will be heightened as you look through life with an intention to create unity.

Even when you fail, you will succeed because you will be more conscious of how you did not create as much unity as was possible. Unfortunately, many people in relationships create constant separation. They may do so unconsciously. As their relationships drift into separation, they are not even aware of the growing distance caused by their being asleep to this love skill. Think of your closest relationships. How could you create more unity and less separation, even in small ways?

As you become more skilled at creating unity, you will see that others feel far more loved in your presence. And they might not even know why – but you will. You will know you chose the softer word, the more uniting idea, or the action that created a higher bond of affection.

Creating unity does not infringe on your independence, nor make you weak. Unity is a powerful position of love leadership and brings great joy to a Love Master's heart. The world is packed with polarization, separation, and divided hearts. We need a new landscape of love. We need to learn and master the skill of seeing and validating our oneness. Unity thinking and acting does this.

Every single time you think, talk, or act in a way that creates unity rather than separation in your relationships, you have expanded the quality of love on our planet. And your relationships will soar. You will experience love on a higher level of living. So will those in your presence.

Unity creates peace. Unity tells us we are loved. Unity causes our hearts to melt. Unity releases our higher gifts. Unity causes us to rise as love beings.

Unity is the enlightened path of a Love Master.

Love Skills Quiz

I create unity rather than separation in my relationships...

1	2	3	4	5	6	7	8	9	10
Never		Seldom		Sometimes			Often		Always

#34
Speak
with Kindness
& Honesty

Kindness & honesty

flowing as one force is the language

of a Love Master

When you speak with kindness and honesty combined, you bring harmony and greater understanding to your relationships – and to yourself.

Kindness & honesty are awesome in their power to create more love. And they need to be expressed *simultaneously* for two good reasons:

- Honesty *without kindness* stings the heart and causes us to retreat.
- Kindness *without honesty* feels empty and untrustworthy and leads away from intimacy.

Expressed together, however, kindness & honesty bring enormous benefits to relationships. We feel safe because of kindness, yet we also feel in touch with another's heart because honesty is also present.

If you are a people pleaser, it takes courage to be honest. If you are accustomed to a direct approach, it takes sensitizing to the importance of kindness.

In an environment of kindness and honesty, intimacy

is vastly increased because people are able to reveal inner desires, hopes, fears, and vulnerable feelings in a supportive & honest environment.

Kindness and honesty flowing as one is the language of a Love Master.

A lack of kindness & honesty is devastating to relationships. We feel disconnected from each other. We feel uncertain. We raise our shields in defense of our fragile dreams and needs. We feel resentment and hurt. In short, we don't feel loved.

These negative consequences are not easily undone. If someone treats us with unkindness in one instance, how can we feel emotionally safe? And if someone is not honest on an issue, how can we believe there will be truth on other issues?

Relationships are fragile. Our dreams, needs, feelings, and ideas are like tiny roots that need tender nourishment. Kindness combined with honesty binds hearts, heals wounds, and uplifts love.

Take honest stock of yourself. Where could you be more kind in your relationships? Where could you be more honest? How could you become better at combining these two love skills? What do you need to let go of?

This is the thinking that is constantly going on inside the heart of a Love Master. Such inner thinking causes your words to flow out to others in harmony with your heart.

The combination of kindness & honesty is one of the potent secrets in the heart of a Love Master.

Love Skills Quiz

I speak with kindness & honesty flowing as one
in my relationships...

1	2	3	4	5	6	7	8	9	10
Never		Seldom		Sometimes			Often		Always

#35

Facilitate

Equality

All hearts are honored

in an environment of equality

Facilitating equality means you champion everyone's right to have equal time to speak, be heard, and be cherished. A lack of equality leaves us feeling socially depleted, overlooked, and wanting something more real.

It takes courage to step up and appoint yourself as a love facilitator, but this is the mark of a Love Master.

Watch the process when several people gather. One person often dominates. Without regard to other's hearts, this person may monopolize. Others don't feel right about interrupting, changing the subject, or creating equality. Everyone is subject to those who dominate – unless a Love Master intervenes with the love skill of facilitating equality. Everyone is glad when this happens!

Here's how it works.

At the very beginning of a gathering, decide to be the one to create equality for everyone. Get the group's attention and suggest that everyone take turns sharing so there can be equality and greater intimacy. Pick an easy or juicy love question and suggest that each person take about three minutes to share from the heart. You might even take the first turn and model it for the others unless someone else is eager to start. It takes practice to get smooth at this, but how much more interesting for a group to share at a heart level with equality than to have stray conversations that leave others out.

A Love Master is highly conscious of each one receiving equal time. You, as a Love Master, are also protective that no one is interrupted or cut short. You can gently intervene when someone interrupts so that the speaker can complete his or her turn.

A great way to proceed after each person has shared is to go another round of sharing. Suggest, perhaps, that each person add something new, or comment on what someone else shared that touched them. They can even share love messages from their hearts about what the entire experience has meant to each of them. Everyone gets another three minutes. And so on.

If someone gets carried away and goes over the time limit, you can, again, be the love facilitator (you are doing everyone else a big favor!) and ask the person softly to bring it to a closing sentence.

Generally, once everyone gets the sense of what the process looks like, no one interrupts. Sometimes, however, someone will forget and begin to have a private conversation aside from the group. As a love facilitator, you can politely ask those people to hold their private conversation until after the group sharing, so everyone gets an opportunity to speak and be acknowledged.

All hearts are fed in an environment of equality. As a Love Master, you know this and take pleasure in creating equality, even when it's not so easy. Others will thank you and learn this love skill through your modeling.

Love Skills Quiz

I facilitate & champion everyone's right to have equal time to speak, be heard, & cherished...

1	2	3	4	5	6	7	8	9	10
Never		Seldom		Sometimes			Often		Always

#36

Flow with Patience

Patience

softens & expands love

Patience is like a magic potion that softens and expands love in relationships.

In our fast-paced, hectic world, relationships often take a dive because patience is so missing. We are being constantly pushed. And we are often stressed, pressured, and pushing ourselves.

During the beginning of a new relationship, patience may flourish easily because both parties are enjoying the newness of love. Once a relationship evolves, however, patience is often a casualty. Tempers can flare.

A Love Master is enormously sensitive to the power of patience to expand love and seeks to keep patience constantly on the love radar.

One way to expand patience in your love relationships is to step outside the view that whatever is happening is an event or task and see it as a "love moment." This moment is exactly what you define it to be.

Thinking of your day as a series of "love moments" enables you to create a flowing path of patience because you understand that the most significant thing going on right now (and now and now) is love.

Of course there are tasks to be completed, and you

may encounter interruptions from others. But seeing these tasks as an opportunity to express patience will get the tasks done with more harmony and your relationships will flourish in the sunshine of your sweet patience.

To become better at expressing patience, create this love intention. Even if you are often impatient, setting the intention to develop your expertise in flowing with patience will expand your relationships to heights you have never imagined.

Think of someone you love who would benefit from your being more patient. The next time you feel impatient, notice what things most tempt you to lose your cool. Plan for success. There is a big payoff in thinking before acting. How could you express more patience to this person? Patience takes awareness and practice.

Love rises dramatically higher in a climate of patience because others feel safe. Hearts relax. Joy and laughter jump to the surface more easily. New ideas emerge more playfully. Defenses drop. Life energy is free to be creative rather than defensive. Harmony expands.

The benefits – to *you* – of being patient are just as wonderful. Finding patience in your heart and actions slows down your life. You find "love meaning" in the present moment. You discover your power to easily create more love in your relationships. You see how your patience dramatically changes the tone and quality of your relationships. You love yourself more. Your relationships evolve to vastly expanded levels of love with deeper trust.

Patience is a soft but powerful love skill used continuously by a Love Master.

Love Skills Quiz

I flow with patience in my relationships...

1	2	3	4	5	6	7	8	9	10
Never		Seldom		Sometimes			Often		Always

#37

Express Joy
& Playfulness

Relationships thrive on
joy & playfulness

Can you laugh at yourself? Are you good at being playful? Can you tease or use sarcasm gently, leaving good feelings with the other person? Can you be goofy or silly? All of these things lead to joy.

Relationships thrive on joy. Having fun and feeling good is essential to a healthy, loving relationship. Have you ever heard a love partner say, "That's enough laughter – let's stop!" No, and you never will! We can't seem to get enough of joy and playfulness.

Expressing joy and playfulness is a decision. What can you do at this moment to lighten up?

As you move towards a lighter place, you become expectant of something to trigger you into joy. If you remain in the expectancy, you will find the universe filling you with joy. Try it.

What tickles your funny place? Will you allow it to occur? Will you agree, in advance, to let go, for even a moment, of your life's burdens and woes and of being in control of things, in order to lighten up, even laugh?

Imagine how more joy will help reduce your body's level of stress and tightness! Imagine what it would do for your day's overall state of happiness. When was the last time you laughed out loud?

What if you decided that you want to have more joy and playfulness, not just for today, but every day? The mere decision to enter the realm of lightness moves you into this happy place.

Make a list of all the reasons you resist joy. As you look at the list, ask yourself, "How much love is this list causing me to lose?" Think of ways you can let go of each and every item on that list to make room for joy. Let yourself get creative. No matter how serious you think something is, how could you add joy?

Here's an example of the power of joy to increase love – and even bring healing. A number of years ago, Shannon accompanied her close girlfriend to the mortuary when her friend's husband suddenly died. Their marriage had been wonderful. On the way, Shannon and her girlfriend, who always giggle and laugh when they are together, started imagining what things could go wrong at the ceremony and they began laughing hysterically about some small, insignificant thing. The tension broke wide open. It felt wonderful at that awful moment in her grief to let her heart break open with laughter. They both decided that he would have liked that for her.

Let your relationships with others be full of joy and playfulness. Even on tough days, humor and joy can save the heart from sadness or despair.

Give yourself a gift today. Allow your heart to be playful. Find humor in whatever is happening. Laugh a lot! Bring joy to others. Feel your joy. Let your joy lighten the load for yourself and for others.

Love Skills Quiz

I express joy & playfulness
in my relationships...

1	2	3	4	5	6	7	8	9	10
Never		Seldom		Sometimes			Often		Always

#38

Forgive
& Move Higher

Forgiveness calls you to rise even higher

as a Love Master in loving others

& yourself

To forgive and move higher is a challenge a Love Master accepts because forgiveness is the way up.

If you listed the people who have caused you the greatest hurt or harm in your life, how many people would make your list? How far back do the hurts go? How deep have the hurts been felt by you? What have they cost you through your repeated memory of the hurt?

Our hurts can be places of great learning. This is the beginning of forgiving and moving higher.

For example, what did you learn from your past hurts? Sometimes we look back and realize we could have spoken up for ourselves, or we could have acted differently, or we could have chosen a better mate or friend in the first place. Hopefully, we have learned how to act differently in order to prevent this type of hurt from occurring again.

Consider this. For the rest of your life, whether or not you see these persons again, you will think of them. Out of the blue, you may think of what they did or said and how it made you feel so hurt.

But right here you have a choice as a Love Master. You

can continue to be the victim of the repeated story in your mind or you can change the story and move higher.

How? You can decide to give your "story" a new outcome. For example, when a past hurt surfaces in your heart, you might reason, "This is exactly where I learned a big lesson on how to love myself better, protect myself, or handle a situation more effectively. I'm glad I've learned that lesson." That's your new story and history! Such redefining strengthens your capacity to move past hurt and enter the door of forgiveness.

And here is a big love truth. Forgiveness is not for the other person. It is primarily for *you!*

Forgiveness cancels your own suffering. The vast majority of reasons why others have hurt you is that they suffer from ignorance. As you call on Love to see their innocence, you feel the first breeze of forgiveness float through your heart.

Forgiveness applies to everyone you feel has ever hurt you, including parents, spouses, friends, and loved ones. Whether or not you believe they deserve your forgiveness is not your concern. *You* deserve the forgiveness in order to release your hurt, grudge, resentment, or pain that will live within you until you begin to think differently about these hurtful times and move higher.

Forgiveness calls you into the role of being a Love Master, being bigger than the problem and willing to rise to a finer you. As challenging as it may be to see someone else as innocent and find genuine, permanent forgiveness in your heart, the struggle to do so will bring peace to your heart – and to your life.

Love Skills Quiz

I forgive those who have hurt me
& move higher...

1	2	3	4	5	6	7	8	9	10
Never		Seldom		Sometimes			Often		Always

#39

Create

Interdependence

Interdependence is the healing, empowering

middle ground between

dependency & independence

Interdependence is a place of exquisite unity where no one loses individuality or power and no one becomes dependent.

Many people in relationships are either highly dependent or highly independent. Interdependence is the healing, empowering middle ground between these two positions.

Interdependency honors each person's desires, needs, feelings, ideas, and ways without letting any party become either submissive or dominating. In interdependent relationships, unity, balance, and love thrive.

Here's how can you create interdependence as a Love Master.

In helping others move away from dependency, begin by seeing them as whole and capable of intelligent thinking and acting. Give them extra opportunities to speak out and share ideas. They may not be accustomed to such self expression, so create the conditions for this to come forth. Move them to the middle ground of equality. Be a catalyst that brings out their talent.

For example, you might say, "You've been very quiet during this discussion. I'd like to fully hear your ideas and recommendations." Or you might say, "You haven't had a opportunity so far to be in charge. Why don't you take the leadership role for awhile. I'd appreciate that."

To help someone move away from domination, gently but firmly move the energy towards middle ground while still honoring the person. You might say, "You've shared lots of good ideas. I'd like to share my ideas now too."

Of course, you yourself may need to move from either dependency or independence to interdependence. Observe yourself with honesty. Have the courage to swing the scale to the middle decisively. Decide to create more love.

If you have been leaning towards independence, you might say, "I've been talking and leading a lot, perhaps too much, and I'd like to support more equal sharing. Would you please take the lead for awhile?"

If you are too dependent, you might say, "I've been rather reserved and allowed you to take the lead. I'd like to have the opportunity for us to share more equally and I'd appreciate your help in giving me that opportunity. I think this will expand our love."

There are many ways to create interdependence. The key is not the words you use, but your attitude. A Love Master's heart is keenly sensitive to moving relationships to the healing place of interdependence. Love flourishes here because all parties are honored. There is more relaxed joy – more discoveries of each other's talents and riches. Love expands.

Love Skills Quiz

I create interdependence, rather than dependency or independence, in my relationships...

1	2	3	4	5	6	7	8	9	10
Never		Seldom		Sometimes			Often		Always

#40

Empower Yourself & Others

Love expands

when everyone is empowered

Empowering yourself and others vastly strengthens loving relationships. Love thrives when all parties are empowered to express their full potential.

It is far too easy for relationships to evolve into roles and habits where one partner drives, one is in charge of money, one is the expert at something else, and one controls the TV remote. This does not expand love.

True empowerment transcends roles and habits.

In our relationship, Shannon pays our bills, but we reconcile our monthly statements together. We both know where the money is – and isn't! Neither of us is in the dark. This creates unity, even in hard times. We both feel financially empowered. Our love is strengthened and expands.

Shannon is an expert healer. It's been her profession for decades. Yet she has always shared her favorite insights about healing so Scott could learn them too. This enabled Scott's healing skills to expand. Her empowering has drawn us closer. Our love has expanded in this shared space of healing.

Scott knows a lot about computers. But rather than simply doing everything himself, he has taught Shannon many skills to develop her computer expertise. As a result, she feels more confident and self-empowered. What might have become a sore point has become a place where we let our love expand through shared skill building.

Sharing your skills with a loved one or friend can be a valuable learning experience and strengthen your relationship. Your success rate with this love skill will be the highest when you use plenty of patience, honoring, and non-judgment. Think of the first goal as creating more love and the second goal as empowerment. Praise the person learning for whatever they are doing well – or even for trying. They will feel grateful for the respect as much as the expanded learning.

If you are not the top talent in some area in your relationship, ask your partner to help you become more talented. Roles dissolve in an empowering climate.

If you are the most talented in another area in the relationship, find ways to let your partner develop this talent too. Learn how to become a great mentor. The tasks may take five times longer to complete at first, but your love will be five times expanded.

Take the attitude of empowering to all your friendships and relationships. What skills do you have that you could share to empower others? Find creative ways to be a mentor or learner. Empowering love creates unity.

As empowerment increases in relationships, equality increases too. Unity blossoms. Hearts feel safer and more honored. Love expands.

A Love Master is on constant lookout for ways to empower everyone!

Love Skills Quiz

I look for ways
to empower myself as well as others...

1	2	3	4	5	6	7	8	9	10
Never		Seldom		Sometimes			Often		Always

Creating

Peace

Creating peace
where
there is conflict
calls forth the deep talents
of a
Love Master

#41

Envision Peace

The first step of a Love Master

in conflict resolution is to

envision peace

To reach peace, we first need to envision peace. This is the starting place for a Love Master dedicated to creating peace where there is conflict.

Conflict creates separation. Peace creates unity.

There is so much suffering due to conflict. Some people will do anything to avoid conflict. Others get immediately inflamed and jump into battle.

What can you do to create peace where there is conflict?

The giant first step is to immediately go inward – before you act or say anything – and envision the highest possibilities for peace. This takes courage, awareness, detachment, and a big commitment to peace.

Conflicts so often seem impossible to solve. Many conflicts have gone on for so long that it's hard to imagine an end to hurt, anger, and hate. Most of us have experienced relationships that try (or fry) our nerves so much that all we can envision is escape or retribution.

It is exactly at this point of "impossibility" that you make the internal decision to create peace. As a Love Master, you know that Love is ultimately the only force that can create true peace so you set in motion a process to get there. This process begins within yourself as you first let go of your own anger, frustration, judgment, and sorrow and begin to ask, "What is the highest possibility of peace that I can envision?"

Asking this question causes you to immediately begin transcending the conflict and see it through higher insight.

It takes courage and strength to refrain from getting engaged in a conflict, to take time to tune in to Love, or Higher Power, and to envision peace from this higher consciousness. Since peace is a higher state of living than conflict, it requires a higher way of thinking.

For example, can you envision an end to a long-standing personal conflict in your life? Can you then go even higher and envision genuine peace? Peace is not just the absence of conflict. Peace is the presence of harmony, understanding, forgiveness, and solutions that are fair and just for all parties. Can you envision this?

That's how a Love Master thinks when presented with conflicts – and it's not pie-in-the-sky hoping. It's a wise, calm, dynamic commitment to a process of creating true peace – no matter how long it takes. Envisioning is the starting place for creating peace. After all, how can people in conflict ever get to a place of genuine peace that cannot even be imagined? Someone needs to envision peace.

Peacemaking requires courage and strength because you are willing to step outside and above the conflict when no one else seems either willing or able. You are willing to envision genuine peace even when it seems like a far-off dream.

This is your beginning stance as a Love Master determined to create peace where there is conflict.

Love Skills Quiz

In conflict, I envision the highest possibility
of peace before acting...

1	2	3	4	5	6	7	8	9	10
Never		Seldom		Sometimes			Often		Always

#42

Set in Motion a Healing Process

Creating peace

is more about the process

than the outcome

Envisioning peace is a huge leap towards peace, but actually getting to peace can be a massive undertaking!

To a Love Master, there is no other path worth choosing than genuine peace. Even if it takes a long, long time to get to peace, that is better than living life in the middle of a never-ending, perpetual conflict.

A Love Master sets in motion a healing *process*. This is a vital principle to understand. *Creating peace is more about the "process" than the "outcome."*

You know that many things need to happen to get to peace:

- Feelings need to get out.
- Good listening needs to take place.
- Judgment and criticism need to be released.
- All parties will eventually need to move past the "story."
- Loving speech will need to emerge.
- Solutions will need to be explored that create unity, justice, and satisfaction.
- There will need to be openings for forgiveness.

- There will need to a peace ending.

That's a lot of *process* that needs to take place on the path to peace, but that is the secret of creating peace. It's all about the process.

A Love Master understands this and sets in motion a healing *process* even though there may be a stalemate, no hope of peace, or even no interest in peace. Outcomes are not the issue. Setting in motion a process is the key.

For example, after envisioning peace in your private thinking and reminding yourself of all the steps that may be needed, you might begin by saying, "I have a vision of peace. Even though it may seem impossible or far off, I'd like to share it." Then ask if they would like to share their vision of peace.

Or you might say, "Let's set in motion some steps that can lead to peace. Why don't you begin by sharing what's in your heart." Or you might say, "I don't want you to suffer any more. I want peace for you. Let's move together to a place of healing and each share our best ideas for creating peace."

It's not about a particular action or the right words. There are many choices. It's about setting a tone and setting in motion a process that can lead to peace.

Your *attitude* of peace as a Love Master sets in motion a healing process.

Love Skills Quiz

In conflict, I begin a *process* to create peace
even though there may seem to be no hope for peace...

1	2	3	4	5	6	7	8	9	10
Never		Seldom		Sometimes			Often		Always

#43

Get

Feelings Out

Peace moves closer when feelings
find an outlet with non-violent expression

Feelings need to get out. In conflict, one side, or both sides, feel victimized. The feelings of anger, hurt, hostility, and even revenge are very real – even explosive.

Peace moves closer when these feelings find an outlet with non-violent expression.

It may not look like peace when someone is venting with emotions, but the road to peace begins with creating an environment where feelings can be freely expressed.

Creating such an environment is essential as a Love Master. The spilling out of feelings is part of a much bigger process leading towards peace – even though it looks far away. Your role is not to squash the feelings, but to create a setting where neither party harms the other.

Even at the worst moment of someone's anger or hurt, let your love presence softly provide leadership.

For example, you might say, "I encourage you to share your feelings. This is a necessary part of healing to let them out. I am going to listen and love you as you do."

Remember, you may not get a polite or loving response back, but it doesn't matter. You are setting the stage for peace. This may be the biggest love test of your day to stay in a place of peace within yourself. Get outside the "moment" or the "words" flying about. You are setting peace in motion. The beginning is never easy.

If you are creating peace between two conflicting parties, you might say, "You are both very upset. I'd like to hear each of your feelings so we can understand each other. Rather than having a verbal duel, let's share one at a time. If it's all right with you, I'll be the peace referee."

Once you make the decision to be a peace maker, stay centered. Remain anchored in moving the peace plot forward. You know that an open sharing of feelings is essential, even if it is not easy or pleasant.

If you happen to be one of the parties in the conflict, well, now the soup gets hotter. It's mighty hard to be part of a conflict and simultaneously be a Love Master determined to create peace. But you can. Peace is always a choice – every single second.

For example, after envisioning what peace might look like as best you can, and gathering as much calmness into your soul as possible, you might say, "I know you are extremely upset. So am I. But I know deep within there is an answer. Let's listen to each other honestly and openly without fighting and with non-violent language. Why don't you share your feelings first and I'll listen without interrupting."

If the other person slips into blaming or condemning, just keep remembering that your goal is to get the feelings out and keep the peace *process* edging forward.

It takes wisdom and patience to get everyone's feelings out, but this is your role as a Love Master.

Love Skills Quiz

In conflict, I create peace by encouraging others to express feelings openly & with non-violent language...

1	2	3	4	5	6	7	8	9	10
Never		Seldom		Sometimes			Often		Always

#44

Listen
with Compassion

Compassionate listening

creates openings

for peace

Conflict needs oxygen to stay alive. It feeds on argument, debate, anger, and reaction.

Compassionate listening has a dramatic ability to create peace in conflict. As soon as you begin listening with compassion and empathy to someone in turmoil, the level of conflict intensity will start to subside.

Hearts need to be heard. Our grief needs to be expressed. Feelings need to be identified, heard, and validated. Thinking needs to be understood and sorted out. Our souls need support.

A Love Master knows these deep needs without even asking and knows that compassionate listening immediately and dramatically reduces conflict.

When those in conflict are listened to with compassion and empathy, there is nothing for their grief, frustration, or anger to feed on. In fact, they feel the first wave of conflict relief – as if there just might be a hint of a solution.

Why?

Because you are listening to their heart. They feel your

compassion and appreciate your empathy.

Listening with compassion does not mean you agree with the person venting or his or her position. You don't take what's being said personally – even if it is meant personally. You see it as simply another point of view that needs to be expressed.

Compassion means that you genuinely care for this person's well being and do not want anyone to suffer.

Because compassion is so vital a love skill, a Love Master seeks to live in a heart space of universal compassion.

Allow your heart to open so wide that you care for everyone on the planet and feel a deep desire to end all suffering. Each individual on this planet deserves to be genuinely loved – including that person you are presently listening to with compassion.

A Love Master brings this consciousness of universal compassion to the present moment, whatever the situation or conflict. You recognize that your compassionate listening in this specific moment is also creating peace on a global level. You are engaged in actively raising the planet's love consciousness and state of love being.

All this is gliding through your awareness as you listen to someone voicing grievances in a conflict mode. He or she will feel your genuine compassion & empathy.

You are actually doing more than listening to intense words being spoken. You are validating that this person's heart and life are of value. He or she will feel your love. Conflict will subside.

Openings for peace will slowly emerge.

Love Skills Quiz

In conflict, I listen with compassion
to all sides...

1	2	3	4	5	6	7	8	9	10
Never		Seldom		Sometimes			Often		Always

#45

Express Unconditional Positive Regard

Unconditional positive regard

transforms hearts & opens doors to peace

When you view others as worthy of love just for being alive and hold them in a space of honoring rather than judgment, you are expressing an attitude of unconditional positive regard.

Unconditional positive regard does not mean you condone a person's actions or agree with a person's position. It does mean, however, that you view this person as deserving to be treated with dignity as a human being. You regard the person in this positive light.

You can even see the core innocence and worth of a person who has wronged you, or who holds a position very opposite to yours.

As a Love Master, you may have to struggle to get there, but this positive attitude towards others creates peace. This also helps you stay in love, living a life of positive regard for all others.

Unconditional positive regard has immense power to transform hearts and open doors to peace.

Others in your presence who experience such unconditional positive regard will find their hearts melting into greater softness because of your love. Their staunch positions on issues will often yield to greater openness because they feel valued by you as a person.

You don't have to agree with what someone says or has done in order for this person to be worthy of your positive regard. Unconditional positive regard transcends words and actions – however mean, harmful, or different – and focuses on every individual as being worthy of love.

For example, let's take a challenging situation. Perhaps there is someone in your life who has been mean or unjust to you. How can you possibly love this person?

Think this through as a Love Master. Unjust or harmful words and actions against you, or anyone else, are unacceptable behavior. They need to cease. The words and actions can legitimately be condemned. But it is the words and actions you are condemning, not the person.

Think of this person when he or she was a one-hour old infant. What if you knew the entire history of what happened to this person from that first moment to today. What would you learn? Was this person abused? Was this person taught to hate? Did this person grow up in conflict? Did this person ever experience being loved? Was this person ever taught the love skills in this book?

As a Love Master, you see the in-born purity of each of us. You understand that people act from ignorance and suffering. You know the underlying solution to conflict is that we all deserve to be respected and loved, not hated.

This is the attitude of unconditional positive regard in the heart of a Love Master.

Love Skills Quiz

In conflict, I treat all parties with unconditional positive regard rather than judgment...

1	2	3	4	5	6	7	8	9	10
Never		Seldom		Sometimes			Often		Always

#46

Be a Loving & Detached Observer

Your presence as a loving, detached observer
will be deeply felt by those
in conflict

Loving detachment during a conflict enables you as a Love Master to stay anchored in inner peace where you can be of higher value to the peace-building process.

To stay detached means that you do not allow yourself to get sucked into the conflict through your own sympathy, frustration, anger, opinion, or point of view.

In a detached mode, you become a better observer. You can see the forest as well as the trees. You can more easily understand other's feelings and points of view from multiple angles of interpretation. You don't feel the need to take sides. Your detached observation enables you to see more clearly the needs and issues behind the story. You are more in an information-gathering mode than a resolution mode.

Being detached as an observer puts you in a stronger place of contribution to peace. Your detachment, however, can come across as being cold and uncaring. That's why it's so important, as a Love Master, to be both loving *and* detached.

For example, if you were detached as an observer but without a loving heart, you might say, "I know we are both upset and feeling angry at each other. But that's just the way it will be until it blows over." This might be an accurate statement, but it would feel cold and unhelpful to those in conflict.

On the other hand, if you were speaking from a place of loving detachment, you might say, "I'm sorry that each of us is suffering. I can see what a toll this is taking on us. But we are both getting our feelings out in the open. This is a healing step and I'm grateful for that."

Your presence as a loving, detached observer will be deeply felt in conflict. Loving detachment from the conflict lowers conflict tension because you, in a true sense, have already transcended the conflict by being both loving and detached. Those in conflict will feel this healing energy.

By being a loving and detached observer, you dramatically affect the peace *process*. Remember, your goal at this point is not a peace outcome or conclusion. The goal, for now, is simply to create an environment of love where the early seeds and tender sprouts of peace can begin to emerge and take root rather than be beaten back down by continuing conflict.

It takes a great deal of mental and heart energy to stay both loving *and* detached. The forces of conflict will perpetually try to drag you in, but, as a Love Master, you understand the peace process.

You know the healing power of being a loving, detached observer.

Love Skills Quiz

In conflict, I am a loving *and* detached observer...

1	2	3	4	5	6	7	8	9	10
Never		Seldom		Sometimes			Often		Always

#47

Encourage
Loving Speech

Loving speech

gently softens hardened hearts

Loving speech is like a soft breeze of love that gently softens hardened hearts.

Getting to loving speech during conflict is a challenge. Both sides are emotionally heated. They use strong, polarizing words such as, "You are an idiot!" "I hate you!" "You are totally wrong!" "I can't believe you could do this to me!" "You've always been this way!"

How do you, as a Love Master on the path of creating peace, help the parties move towards more loving speech?

Primarily by your own example.

Every sentence that comes out of your mouth can be full of words that convey peace.

Rather than saying, "Would you just shut up and suggest a solution," you might say, "We've got some strong feelings here and that's a healthy part of getting to eventual peace. As challenging as it may be, let's work through these issues with words that allow us to find genuine solutions without harming each other."

As a Love Master helping to create peace, you know it may take many rounds of harsh words that will need to be re-expressed by you – in a softened, loving tone – to bring everyone to loving speech. You are the model in this stage of the peace process – and most likely the only model.

Loving speech softly but effectively infiltrates anger and division. Negative energy slowly dissolves when greeted by your persistently loving speech.

If you are a party to the conflict and you are trying your hardest to be a Love Master midst your own strong feelings, congratulations. Your *motive* is shifting the process towards peace.

You might find yourself saying, "I'm trying very hard to get past my anger and hurt and use words that will create unity rather than separation, so please bear with me. I genuinely want us to find peace." This is an example of honest, loving speech rather than inflammatory, attacking words.

Loving speech has surprising results. To the extent that you use words that unify rather than separate, the conflict will begin to diffuse right in front of you. This is the extraordinary power of loving speech. "Tough" language doesn't stand a chance against a persistent barrage of heart-felt loving speech. Separation begins to crumble.

No, you are not yet at the end point of peace just because speech is more loving. But you have dramatically shifted the energy to the side of peace. You are on the way. It's all about the *process*.

That's the secret in a Love Master's heart. That's also why you won't run out of patience – because you know that peace is inevitable if you stay the course of loving speech.

Love Skills Quiz

In conflict, I express & encourage loving speech…

1	2	3	4	5	6	7	8	9	10
Never		Seldom		Sometimes			Often		Always

#48

Gently Move Past "the Story"

When those in conflict
move past their "story," new openings
for peace emerge

Moving past the "story" can be a major hurdle in creating peace.

In conflict, there is always a "story." Each side feels wronged. Each side feels justified. Each side knows the "facts." Both sides have rehearsed and retold their versions of the "story" many times. Some stories seem hard, almost impossible, to let go.

This is exactly where you step even further into the peace process as a Love Master. You know these stories must be told. They need to be vented and emotionally released. The "story" needs to be heard and understood.

But once that happens, then what?

Then you gently guide those in conflict to move past their story. The key word here is "gently." There's no rush. Creating peace, remember, is a process more than an outcome. Focus on the *process*.

For eventual, true peace, of course, there will need to be forgiveness and solutions for unity and justice. But for now, in this new tender moment, after someone's "story" has been heard, there is an opening, however slight, for moving past the story into deeper peace.

So, for example, you might say, "Thank you for sharing your experience. It's valuable to hear and understand your point of view. I'm glad you've expressed it so fully and openly. I imagine you feel some relief just getting it out so clearly." And then, after reflecting back so they know you heard them accurately, you might say to them, "Even though it may seem far off, what do you envision as the next step towards peace?"

This, of course, is a loaded question and may take you on another ride of the "story," but the question is also speaking to the other person's Highest Self and offering an invitation to higher ground.

Suppose the person says, "I have no idea what the next step is. There is no solution." This is OK. The peace process is gently unfolding. There is at least a discussion now of what a "next step" might be. You have successfully and gently moved past the "story."

You might say. "I know it seems impossible to imagine a solution, but I believe in my heart that there is one and I'm going to stick with you until we find it." And the *process* of peace moves forward another emotional inch.

The words on this page are only samples. Let Love put the perfect words of peace in your heart. Those in conflict will feel your heart genuinely caring for their suffering. They will feel your commitment to seeking real peace.

You are not forcing peace on anyone, but creating an environment for peace to naturally emerge. This is the patient, sometimes invisible, work of a Love Master in the midst of creating peace.

Love Skills Quiz

In conflict, I help get everyone's "story" out in the open & then help them gently move past their story...

1	2	3	4	5	6	7	8	9	10
Never		Seldom		Sometimes			Often		Always

#49

Explore Solutions for Unity & Justice

An exploration of solutions

for unity & justice

creates opportunities for genuine peace

The goal in conflict resolution is not just to end conflict. The higher goal is to create peace based on unity and justice.

Stand back now and see what has already happened in the peace-building process.

Your influence as a Love Master has gently moved people through the process of getting their feelings out. They have been listened to with compassion and cared for with unconditional positive regard. You have helped them gently move past the "story" with communication that is now tilted towards loving speech rather than conflict vocabulary. This is major peace progress, even without a final solution – *because the process of peace building is as important as any final solution.*

True peace is not a final contract or agreement, but a way of living based on unity and justice.

With all you have accomplished as a Love Master, you can now use your influence to help explore solutions for unity and justice. This takes expertise because the parties may not be ready to explore solutions.

For example, if you are a party in the conflict, you might articulate the other person's needs with loving speech and accuracy, and then summarize your own needs with the same accuracy and neutral observation. Then you might say, "I think we understand each other's needs more clearly. Let's take turns and explore solutions that will create unity and feel fair to each of us. Would you like to start?"

Things may not go smoothly, but you are vastly shifting the peace process to higher ground by bringing the focus to an exploration of solutions.

As a Love Master, you are keenly aware that those in conflict feel that a great injustice has been done to them. So you don't side step the issues of unity and justice for a more superficial end to conflict. You are willing to explore what will truly create unity and justice.

You might dive in and say, "As I've been listening to each of our feelings and needs, I can see how differently this issue looks to each of us. Yet I can also see the innocence of our hearts and our openness for a higher solution. It may take a lot of work, but let's explore possible solutions for unity and justice together."

As a Love Master, you are not imposing or forcing a peace solution on anyone. You are simply opening the door to an exploration of solutions for genuine peace based on unity and justice.

Even if this exploration door keeps closing or jamming, you keep opening it. You know that getting to unity and justice is what is needed for real peace. You constantly remember that peace is a process.

Love Skills Quiz

In conflict, I help all parties explore solutions
for unity and justice...

1	2	3	4	5	6	7	8	9	10
Never		Seldom		Sometimes			Often		Always

#50

Create Openings
for Forgiveness

*Forgiveness becomes easier when
you understand another's innate innocence*

Forgiveness is the final frontier in the peace-building
process.

As a Love Master involved in a creating peace, let's
review forgiveness:

- Forgiveness does not mean that someone
  condones another's wrongful or harmful
  actions.
- Forgiveness does not depend on both parties
  forgiving. One party can forgive alone.
- Mutual forgiveness based on understanding of
  each other's needs and a true desire for fairness
  is the highest place of peace.

Even though the possibility of forgiveness may seem
distant or even impossible, a Love Master gently, but
constantly creates openings for forgiveness. Forgiveness
may occur slowly and in small ways, but each opening for
forgiveness moves the process of peace to higher ground.

Forgiveness in conflict is far more than getting one
side to admit they were wrong and then apologize so the
other side can forgive them.

Forgiveness is for everyone involved. Once a person in a
conflict moves into an attitude of forgiveness, that person's

heart will find immense healing and relief. Our hearts yearn to live in peace and unity. Conflict is antagonistic to our well being. When we move to forgiveness, the walls of separation slip towards unity. Forgiveness seals peace within our own heart.

A key to the process of creating openings for forgiveness is to understand the innate innocence of each party. When you dig deep for the cause of harmful actions and words in a conflict, you will usually discover that the real cause of conflict is ignorance, a lack of being genuinely loved, as well as a lack of experiencing or being taught the love skills in this book.

Forgiveness becomes easier when you understand someone's views. It's not easy to do this in the middle of anger, meanness, or injustice, but that's your role as a Love Master. And not just to see this yourself, but to help all sides in the conflict get glimpses of each other's needs.

Your goal as a peacemaker is not to force anyone to forgive. Your focus is to keep the process of peace moving steadily forward. You have done this with your calm, empathetic listening and unconditional positive regard. And you have done this by gently exploring solutions for unity and justice satisfying for everyone.

At this stage of peace-building, you are taking advantage of the greater goodwill that the peace process has created to explore forgiveness. Healing solutions and attitudes almost sneak into reality because of your confidence in the peace process as a Love Master.

Love Skills Quiz

In conflict, I create gentle, but constant openings
for forgiveness...

1	2	3	4	5	6	7	8	9	10
Never		Seldom		Sometimes			Often		Always

#51

Create

A Peace Ending

A Love Master creates peace endings

even if peace has not yet arrived

A true peace ending is the continuation of the *process* of peace rather than a specific outcome.

Even if parties in conflict reach an agreement to resolve a conflict, that does not necessarily mean they have arrived at peace. They may still be wary of each other. They may still distrust. They may still be on high alert. They may still be far from forgiveness. Or unity.

As a Love Master, you know this. You know that real peace is just beginning to take hold. You also know that if steady, open, and honoring communication continues, peace will move from "tentative" to "genuine."

Even though conflict may have come to an end, the process of peace building continues.

So you might say to the parties involved, "I'm grateful we have moved to the place of ending the conflict. How do you feel now? What steps do you feel would lead to sustained and lasting peace?"

These are loaded love questions that may poke at smoldering hurts and cause sparks, but this is the courage needed to move the process from an end to conflict to the creation of genuine peace.

No matter how the parties respond, you and they are

now fully engaged in creating a peace ending. Genuine peace requires lots of reassuring words and actions. Many of these words and actions have come from you in the role of peace builder. Now these words and actions can more easily come from the other parties too. Encourage all parties to express their own peace endings too.

What if you are personally involved in a conflict but want to create a peace ending yourself as a Love Master?

This intention alone moves the conflict towards genuine peace. You might say, "We've each done a lot of talking and listening to each other and we've each suggested solutions for unity and justice. I know we are still upset within our hearts, but I'd like to find a way of truly ending this conflict and moving to genuine peace. Can we discuss this?"

Here's a big moment of truth. Even though you are creating openings for a peace ending, others may not be ready. That's OK. You haven't failed. You have succeeded because you are furthering the *process* of peace.

Don't lose confidence in the process. Remind yourself that you are dedicated, as a Love Master, to unconditional positive regard. That's a big commitment, but that's the secret of creating genuine peace.

Even if parties decide to leave still short of genuine peace, you might say, "I'm glad we've all been so open and come so far. I'm committed to staying the course of peace and I'm going to continue holding the space for peace in my heart even when we part. I hope you will too."

Creating peace endings that continue the *process* of creating peace is one of the secrets of a Love Master.

Love Skills Quiz

In conflict, I gently but consistently
create peace endings...

1	2	3	4	5	6	7	8	9	10
Never		Seldom		Sometimes			Often		Always

Healing

with

Love

The
final destination
of
Love
is
healing

#52

Ask Love

As you become quiet and still,

tuning in to Love,

you become the knower of healing answers

You can ask Love for healing answers for anything and everything of concern in your life.

When you operate in partnership, you check in with your partner. Each partner brings the very best to each other. If you think your partner knows more than you do, it's smart to ask questions of your partner so you can enjoy the benefits of this wisdom.

This is the opportunity you have with Love Itself. Consider Love (or Higher Power) to be your life partner. This Source is the sum of all the love that has ever existed. This same Source is your Love partner and an infinite resource to help you create and experience more love.

If you could ask Love anything right now, what would you ask?

For example, you could ask for understanding and direction in a relationship, comfort for a hurt you have experienced in the past, encouragement to go forward in more love, and guidance in how to do this. You can ask Love anything your heart desires or needs to know.

Pause a moment and ask Love something you would consider helpful to know.

Now that you have asked Love, how will you know

Love's answer?

Love has endless ways of communicating to you so you will receive and understand its healing answer. Love awakens thoughts, feelings, images, and mental pictures within you and offers immense divine influence for you to receive all the help you ask for.

We often miss Love's answers because we forget to listen to Love for the answer even though we've asked Love a question. Yet we would never consider taking a road trip, asking for directions, and then neglecting to listen carefully for the directions!

Something unusual occurs when we ask Love for an answer. Since Love doesn't have a human voice and doesn't write us emails, we need to prepare ourselves to receive information in a new and higher way.

As you become quiet and still, tuning in to Love, you become the knower of healing answers. They may come through an inner feeling or a new understanding of things that you didn't have before you asked. Or healing answers may come in the most surprising and unexpected way. Be assured, however, that every time you ask Love, you will receive an answer.

Asking Love also enables you to be prepared for difficult moments or situations because asking Love gives you instant access to Love's power, protection, inspiration, and healing wisdom.

Your closest partner, Love, is always with you and tuned in to you with endless love. From this state of high Love alignment, you become a natural channel for healing – for yourself and for others.

Love Skills Quiz

I ask Love (or Higher Power) for
healing answers...

1	2	3	4	5	6	7	8	9	10
Never		Seldom		Sometimes			Often		Always

#53

Flood
with Comfort

As a Love Master,

you can bring Love's flood of comfort

to everyone you know

What would it feel like for you to be flooded with comfort right now? How would it change how you presently feel?

From the moment comfort arrives, our hearts feel swept with relief. We begin to let go of fears, anxiety, burdens, and doubts tightly held within. Comfort brings soothing ease from stress. It brings hope to areas that lie in hopelessness. Any troubled area receives immediate attention. Worry begins to leave. Uneasy feelings are replaced with positive openings.

Don't you wish this for everyone in the world? Don't you believe that most everyone would welcome the experience of such full comfort? We all need more of Love's healing comfort.

As a Love Master, you can bring Love's flood of comfort to everyone you know. This doesn't place you higher than others, nor does it assume you look down on others as though to pity their weakness. And it doesn't make you their teacher or adviser. A comforter is one who serves another's needs and offers something loving to gently help the other person.

As a comforter, you are Love's fresh waters, alleviating any fear, worry, or pain that the person might be experiencing. This doesn't mean you must fix their problem, only to bring comfort.

Others may never know that you are intentionally offering them comfort. But a Love Master is called into the action of comfort whenever others are speaking their stress, worry, fear, or doubt.

As a Love Master, listen for your cue. Find ways to offer comfort that others can happily receive so they can feel wonderful about themselves and reunited with Love.

Here are examples of words you might share to offer comfort with others:

- "What's going on in your life right now? I'd love to know and be closer to you."
- "You look sad today. Would you like to share with me what's going on in your heart?"
- "I'm so sorry you are unhappy. How can I help you feel better?"
- "Thank you for being so open. I understand how you feel."
- "I'm going to hold a high thought for you and envision Love bringing all the comfort you need."
- "I want you to know that I care about you and wish great joy for you."

Statements like these speak directly to another's heart and bring deep comfort. Others will feel your love.

Love Skills Quiz

I bring divine Love's flood of comfort
to everyone I know...

1	2	3	4	5	6	7	8	9	10
Never		Seldom		Sometimes			Often		Always

#54

Speak

As Love

The moment you speak as Love Itself,

you bring forth healing

Speaking as Love means that you let Love (or Higher Power) put the words in your heart and you then voice these words to others. In short, Love is speaking directly to the other person through you.

When we see someone suffering, our hearts yearn to speak up. Even if there is no suffering, our hearts want to be even closer to our loved ones. But what do we say?

We let Love speak – through us. Who would enjoy hearing Love speak to them through you?

When you tune in intuitively and ask Love what to say, something very surprising occurs. You become aware that Love does indeed have something to say and it can be said by you! Such lovely heart talk can occur anytime and all you want, not just in times of suffering.

As a Love Master, you have passed the point of quietly thinking thoughts that are never uttered. As a natural Love healer, you share these comforting thoughts that reveal how you feel and bring love to the present moment. This is healing.

Most people ignore Love's voice within, doubting that it is correct, or that anyone would want to hear it, or that they could deliver Love's message with success. Yet Love wants to be known and seen and felt on every occasion. Love wants each of us to be part of speaking as Love.

As you practice this love skill of speaking as Love, you will come to trust your intuition in hearing Love.

By making the assumption that Love is communicating at all times, you can pick up on Love's messages and deliver them as often as you like. You can even begin your sharing with, "What Love is telling me to say to you is..." and then speak exactly what comes to you. It can be simple and sweet. It can be a lovely mental picture you receive through inspiration, even when the other person is talking. Love will show you how to do this.

How do you know it is from Love? You know because it will feel right. It will be loving, sweet, uplifting, and inspired. Love may even have you share a caring thought that best describes how you feel as you spend time with someone. Imagine being connected with others through Love itself!

Consider what occurs when someone speaks as Love, however long the speaking occurs. The power of Love is invited to sit with you both and creates a moment of great healing. Who is more qualified than Love to do this!

Imagine writing a love note to someone and letting Love write the note! Others will read something far deeper than the words. They will be touched with healing. This is a wonderful way to bring your sweetest love intention to others. They will want you to speak Love to them often. They may even be encouraged to speak as Love to you!

A Love Master is fluent in speaking *as* Love.

Love Skills Quiz

I listen intuitively to Love & let Love (or Higher Power) speak through me to others...

1	2	3	4	5	6	7	8	9	10
Never		Seldom		Sometimes			Often		Always

#55

Call Forth the Divine

*By calling forth the divine
in yourself & others,
you step into the shoes of a healer*

When you look at someone, what do you see? As a Love Master, you realize the enormous power of seeing past appearances and your feelings about someone in order to see the divine in them.

Think of yourself as a Love viewer. You can choose how you view others. In some cases, viewing the divine in someone may mean that you must first rise above your differences or hurts. It means you will take your view of them to Love's highest plane, the divine. When you do, wonderful things occur. This is the highest place you can go as a Love Master.

How do you view someone as divine? First, think of the source of all love. By its nature, Love is divine. Love is the creator of itself. Love is also completely present and everywhere at once. Begin to realize that this everywhere-at-once status is true as we view ourselves and others.

In order to view everything, everywhere as Love, it takes practice to see Love supplant the mixed view of yourself and your mixed view of others. You may not see Love with your physical eyes, but you know Love is always present and you can call on its Presence anytime you desire. Let the invisible come into view as you call forth the divine in yourself and others with quiet authority and conviction.

This dramatically changes all your relationships. Although you have close relationships with people you love, your primary relationship is with Love itself. Your determination to see Love everywhere, above all else, is the method by which you will also be calling it forth.

Your divine view of others not only silently calls forth the divine in them, but it is also powerful for healing.

Wouldn't you like others to see your divinity? Their view would call forth your Highest Self. What do you think would happen? Healing!

The final destination of Love is healing. In this divine place, you are directed by Love to invoke Love's healing power. You become Love's authorized healer, enabling Love to be known in amazing and incalculable ways.

Think what a wonderful opportunity you have to view the divine within yourself and all others and allow this to call forth all wonderful blessings for you and them today! What a purpose for your life!

Each time or occasion you speak your divine view of another, calling forth the divine, you do it for everyone. This brings immense healing. Could there be anything more rewarding?

This is why, as you practice living as a Love Master, you become a natural healer.

Love Skills Quiz

I call forth the divine in myself & others...

1	2	3	4	5	6	7	8	9	10
Never		Seldom		Sometimes			Often		Always

#56
Offer
Sweet Assurance

Sweet assurances from Love

comfort our hearts

& tell us we are cherished & worthy

Sweet assurances tell us that we are whole, valuable, liked, loved, and cared for. Assurances are healing because they inspire confidence and certainty. Every single person on this planet needs sweet assurance.

What do we most want to hear that would silence the uncertainties we face and the outcomes we fear? We want to know that all is well, that things are going to work out, and that we are going to be fine.

This is exactly the message that Love brings to each heart. As a Love Master, you have the wonderful opportunity to give these sweet assurances, speaking as Love Itself. Even though divine assurances may be rarely uttered in your life or with your friends, a Love Master knows their healing effect and is not afraid to voice Love's assurances.

Love puts an end to our most outrageous anxieties about ourselves – our positions, relationships, money, jobs, health, and futures. An assuring arm around us, a hug, or Love's words uttered all act to tell us we are cared for by Love, cherished and worthy, and that we are going to be all right. The entire nervous system takes a deep breath of rest at that moment. Joy can re-enter. Feelings of wellness and strength return. An assured life is the optimum life. Sweet assurances meet a basic need for love, every day.

Why don't we offer these simple assurances to ourselves and others? Perhaps we are numb to the inner chatter of fear and anxiety. Our daily insecurities may seem natural rather than unnatural. Perhaps we gave up trying to fight the feeling of an inevitable downward gravitational pull in life. Look at how much joy is at stake!

As a Love Master, you offer Love's sweet assurances to your friends and even to those you may not know. By doing so, you bring forward love that immediately offers healing. Think of how many ways there are to say, "My heart is with you," "You are precious and valued and Love will never let you down," or "I'm holding the space for all healing for you today."

It is more than just words. A Love Master looks deep within the person and sees the strength, even if the strength is lying there asleep. A Love Master calls forth this strength into action!

Sweet assurances are based on the powerful inner resources that lie within each of us when we are in Love alignment. The assurances that Love conveys through you have the authority and healing power of Love.

Feel the sweet assurance from Love to you right now that you are a capable, wonderful, and treasured Love Master.

Love Skills Quiz

I offer sweet assurances to my friends
& even people I don't know...

1	2	3	4	5	6	7	8	9	10
Never		Seldom		Sometimes			Often		Always

#57

Praise Generously
& Often

Praising generously & often
causes others to feel deeply loved & valued

When a Love Master sees something wonderful in others, he or she gives them the longer, more enthusiastic version of praise. How do you feel when someone offers you generous praise?

Generous praise comes deeply from the heart and expresses genuine, enthusiastic appreciation. Praising generously and often causes others to feel deeply loved and valued. Love overflows. Hearts feel nurtured.

Most people don't give generous praise. Nor do they praise often. This is a sad loss of love for all of us.

Yet by giving generous love, we also receive it. How many people do you know who would turn down praise?

Praise validates that our efforts to improve and be the best version of ourselves is being noticed and is working. When we receive positive, thorough acknowledgment, we often suddenly realize how starved we were to hear something good about ourselves.

Since we so often carry negative, inner self talk, it is immediately relieving, refreshing, and encouraging to feel appreciated, even complimented. It adds to our sense of self worth to hear that someone appreciates us. Joy enters our heart. It is healing. How often would you like to have this experience? How often do you give this experience?

Generous praise comes from your gratitude and overflow. When you praise generously, it has a healing effect on you as well as the other person. A day of praising – people, events, and whatever might be overlooked or taken for granted – means you create a day full of love. You can create a new habit to do this every day!

Generous praise represents the highest you. It means you are big enough and connected enough to Love to be free and unrestrained with your gifts of acknowledgment. It means you have stepped beyond petty considerations of smallness, stinginess, self concern, and the need to also receive in return. It means you can love unconditionally in this moment rather than judging or criticizing. It means you can make a big difference in other's lives today.

As a Love Master, you can be so good at frequent, generous praise that others will be happily expectant of a love wave coming from your heart when they see you!

Some people don't receive praise easily. That's okay. Don't let that stop you. They need and want it anyway. Perhaps your sincere words will open their hearts to not only receive more love, but to recognize the value of generous praise and to offer it to others themselves.

What if every person on the planet generously praised two people today? What would be the healing effect? We would all be part of creating twice as much love! A Love Master is always looking for opportunities to praise.

By the way, thank you for your wonderful desire to be a Love Master yourself. We applaud your lovely heart!

Love Skills Quiz

I praise others often & generously...

1	2	3	4	5	6	7	8	9	10
Never		Seldom		Sometimes			Often		Always

#58

Resonate with Love

Love causes you

to resonate in harmony

with others

There is a sympathetic Love vibration within each of us. When we hear and know our unique, individual sound, we long to take our place and connect with other sounds.

There is a chord of love that wants to be heard in our deepest soul. We know that we cannot create the symphony alone. It requires others. But it also requires us. There are many notes. Many chords. But one symphonic sound.

The beauty of the collective music that blends together in a universal love symphony causes us to resonate in oneness. Our unified oneness is felt in the spheres as a song of Love, singing itself to the universe. We are home.

This is what we most have in common at the deepest level of our souls. We know when the chord is being sung and when we are called to take our place within the notes so perfectly attuned. The exquisite beauty is masterful. It is enthralling to our soul.

As you sit alone, perhaps quietly reading this book, become aware of the universal resonance of which you are a part. It is Love resonating between us right now

– and with all others. Feel it in your heart.

There is an energy current of love that flows through each of us. It runs at a frequency pitch that calls us into it, to sing our note. We are meant to resonate with each other and to live in Love's resonance.

Feel your vibration. By feeling your own vibration and sensing your note, you not only join others but you also hold the structure for many others to recognize the call so they too can sing their note. Your note is a calling to others to join you.

A Love Master has deep sensing skills of resonance.

Who do you most resonate with that you know? Who is someone in history you most resonate with and why?

Become aware of when you are resonating. Notice the feeling. Memorize the vibration frequency. It is the resonance of Love.

It is where you operate in a non-local way. It is your universal self acting itself out through love resonance. It has intelligence to know things. Tap into this vast reservoir of information leading your life and connecting you with others like you.

Think of yourself as being in Love's healing symphony. What is Love's song that we are singing together? What is your part?

You are having an immense healing affect on the entire universe as you resonate in Love.

Thank you for tuning in and singing your beautiful notes.

Love Skills Quiz

I feel Love (or Higher Power) causing me to resonate in harmony with others...

1	2	3	4	5	6	7	8	9	10
Never		Seldom		Sometimes			Often		Always

#59

Hold the Space
for Healing

*Holding the space for healing
is your high position as a Love Master*

L ove is the healer. As a Love Master, you know this. It is the power of divine Love that heals.

Your job is to turn to Love and hold a mental space open for Love to work through you. It is an easy process when you focus and allow this to happen.

Then why does life seem to be so hard? Disturbances arise when you deal with inner thoughts that conflict with Love's peace. Which reality will you choose? Disturbances or divine Love? Your higher choice creates healing.

During any onslaught of problems for yourself or others, "hold the space for healing" as a Love Master. In other words, maintain your direct, personal relationship with Love and listen deeply for Love's guidance. It will come. Know all will be well. Take the position that, until this evidence shows up, you are going to hold the space for healing for yourself and for others. Love is with you.

From this position of steady faith and holding the space open for healing, negative thoughts are eventually released and healing occurs.

Love is the creator of everything that exists, and Love is all present. Love is never absent. There is no place or space that Love does not already occupy.

Even where there is great concern or fear, Love is there. Think of it! All space in every moment is already filled with Love – regardless of appearances. As a Love Master healer, you are holding your mental space open for this truth to be more realized by yourself and others.

View yourself as one who is stationed at the door of Love. Your job is to keep the door open. Through this doorway pours all light, joy, strength, healing, love, peace, pureness, innocence, understanding, power, beauty, energy, vision, inspiration, wisdom, action, and divinity.

Notice that whenever you have negative thoughts or images, your Love doorway appears to close. But as you remember Love's presence and power, you watch Love outshine the negativity, and the doorway opens once again. Love's reality prevails!

If you feel discouraged, worried, or afraid that you don't feel or see Love, look at these thoughts as "door closing thoughts." Keep the door open. Hold the space for Love. Soon you will see Love again – and experience Love's healing effects.

Love presents wonderful and infinite possibilities to us in every moment. How many of these possibilities are you open to? How long can you stay open to these possibilities? This is the place of a healer.

When anyone says that something is wrong and tells you why, you can respond with great compassion but also hold the space open for Love's wonderful and infinite possibilities. Keep the door wide open.

This is your high and healing position as a Love Master.

Love Skills Quiz

When faced with problems for myself or others, I hold the space for healing by Love (or Higher Power)...

1	2	3	4	5	6	7	8	9	10
Never		Seldom		Sometimes			Often		Always

Leaving
A Trail of
Love

*Parting in love
leaves a
sweet trail
of love
for
eternity*

#60

Leave a
Love Imprint

A Love Master's parting
leaves a sweet trail of love that
uplifts & endures

Saying goodbye gives a Love Master a wonderful opportunity to leave an imprint of love that uplifts and endures.

Think of the last person you were with. How did you feel after you parted? Did he or she leave an imprint of love behind that felt sweet and uplifting to your heart?

And, of course, did you leave an imprint of sweet love that caused this person to feel loved and special?

Your intention to say goodbye with good feelings causes you to be alert in partings. Rather than casually thinking you will see someone again soon – or that you might never see this person again anyway – you see each parting as a magnificent love opportunity.

As a Love Master, you know how deeply a parting remains with someone so you take special care of other's hearts as you part.

Here are some possible ways to say goodbye that create wonderful feelings as you part:

- "It's been wonderful seeing you. I hope you have a very special and love-filled day."

- "I enjoyed our time together a lot and I look forward to being with you again."
- "Thank you for who you are. You are such a treasure. I hope you know that."
- I know we're saying goodbye for now, but I'll be thinking of you with a lot of love today."

Such partings are genuine and memorably sweet, not mediocre or fizzling out. They all say, "I love you." And why not? Why not love everyone? And why not say it?

This is how a Love Master creates love at a parting. There isn't a feeling of separation. There is a feeling of unity and continuity. Even after parting, others feel the permanent residue of your love. They feel your caring. They feel uplifted just remembering your presence.

Rather than taking it for granted that someone already knows you like or love them, let it be spoken and heard. Have you ever doubted whether someone liked you because he or she was not good at showing or stating it?

A Love Master speaks up openly and fully at partings, knowing how meaningful simple sentiments from the heart can be. We all need to hear more love words spoken.

It is such good news to hear that someone cares for you – to hear clear words of love that are memorable with sweetness. This is the parting we all deserve. As a Love Master, you can set the example. Your heart will feel better doing this – and you'll find many others will return a sweet love parting.

Thank you for reading this book. We hope *you* feel our continuing love and our admiration for every step you take to live as a Love Master. We cherish who you are!

Love Skills Quiz

When parting from others, I leave a love imprint that uplifts & endures...

1	2	3	4	5	6	7	8	9	10
Never		Seldom		Sometimes			Often		Always

Appendix

Love Skills Quiz

This **Love Skills Quiz** is designed to quickly reveal your love strengths & needs. Just by taking this quiz, your love skills will begin to expand.

For each of the 60 questions, rate yourself from 1 to 10. If you go with your first instinct, the quiz will only take a few minutes. If you are debating between two numbers, go with the higher one. That's part of loving yourself. You can have only one rating for each question, but you can change your rating at anytime. Be sure to answer each question.

At the end of the quiz, go back and (1) add up your total score and (2) divide that by 60. That will give you your average **Love Skills Score.** There is a revealing interpretation of your score at the end of the quiz.

Section 1
Grounding Yourself in Love

(There is only one question in Section 1)

1. Love flows through me as I think, feel, speak, & act...

1	2	3	4	5	6	7	8	9	10
Never		Seldom		Sometimes			Often		Always

Continued on next page

Section 2
Loving Yourself

2.   I receive love generously...

    1   2   3   4   5   6   7   8   9   10
  Never   Seldom   Sometimes   Often   Always

3.   I know & cherish my life purpose...

    1   2   3   4   5   6   7   8   9   10
  Never   Seldom   Sometimes   Often   Always

4.   I give myself sacred solitude so I can be still & listen to Love (or Higher Power) for guidance...

    1   2   3   4   5   6   7   8   9   10
  Never   Seldom   Sometimes   Often   Always

5.   I honor & validate my feelings...

    1   2   3   4   5   6   7   8   9   10
  Never   Seldom   Sometimes   Often   Always

6.   I see & love myself as a masterpiece unfolding ...

    1   2   3   4   5   6   7   8   9   10
  Never   Seldom   Sometimes   Often   Always

7.   I practice positive inner love talk as a healthy way of loving myself well...

    1   2   3   4   5   6   7   8   9   10
  Never   Seldom   Sometimes   Often   Always

8. I love my body & appreciate its value in helping me fulfill my life purpose...

1	2	3	4	5	6	7	8	9	10
Never		Seldom		Sometimes			Often		Always

9. I am fully visible to myself and to others and I allow myself freedom to be me...

1	2	3	4	5	6	7	8	9	10
Never		Seldom		Sometimes			Often		Always

10. I set healthy boundaries that honor my needs as just as important as other's needs...

1	2	3	4	5	6	7	8	9	10
Never		Seldom		Sometimes			Often		Always

11. I forgive myself, knowing that I am learning and growing and becoming a more enlightened person...

1	2	3	4	5	6	7	8	9	10
Never		Seldom		Sometimes			Often		Always

Section 3
Greeting Others With Love

12. I set a clear love intention before I greet someone...

1	2	3	4	5	6	7	8	9	10
Never		Seldom		Sometimes			Often		Always

13. When greeting others, I smile openly, generously, & genuinely...

1	2	3	4	5	6	7	8	9	10
Never		Seldom		Sometimes			Often		Always

14. When greeting others, I look directly, but softly, into their eyes & hold this contact for a few seconds...

1	2	3	4	5	6	7	8	9	10
Never		Seldom		Sometimes		Often		Always	

15. When greeting others, I hug them with an open heart, but also with a keen sensitivity to their needs...

1	2	3	4	5	6	7	8	9	10
Never		Seldom		Sometimes		Often		Always	

16. When greeting someone, I voice a short but genuine love message so he or she will feel loved...

1	2	3	4	5	6	7	8	9	10
Never		Seldom		Sometimes		Often		Always	

Section 4
Creating Intimacy

17. I am proactive & take the lead in creating genuine intimacy when I am with someone...

1	2	3	4	5	6	7	8	9	10
Never		Seldom		Sometimes		Often		Always	

18. When I am with someone, I am present & tuned in, focusing on the vast potential of love in the moment...

1	2	3	4	5	6	7	8	9	10
Never		Seldom		Sometimes		Often		Always	

19. When I am with someone, I ask "love questions" such as "What are you most passionate about?...

1	2	3	4	5	6	7	8	9	10
Never		Seldom		Sometimes		Often		Always	

20. When someone is speaking from the heart, I listen with empathy...

1 2 3 4 5 6 7 8 9 10
Never Seldom Sometimes Often Always

21. I accept others without judgment...

1 2 3 4 5 6 7 8 9 10
Never Seldom Sometimes Often Always

22. When I am listening, I use silence as a tool of love...

1 2 3 4 5 6 7 8 9 10
Never Seldom Sometimes Often Always

23. When listening & someone finishes a thought & pauses, I encouragingly say, "Tell me more..."

1 2 3 4 5 6 7 8 9 10
Never Seldom Sometimes Often Always

24. After listening, I reflect back what I have heard in order to validate the accuracy of my listening...

1 2 3 4 5 6 7 8 9 10
Never Seldom Sometimes Often Always

25. After listening to others, I honor their soul by telling them how special & valuable they are...

1 2 3 4 5 6 7 8 9 10
Never Seldom Sometimes Often Always

26. I am transparent (open) when I am communicating with others...

1 2 3 4 5 6 7 8 9 10
Never Seldom Sometimes Often Always

27. I speak with gentleness to soothe hearts & allow intimacy to flow...

1	2	3	4	5	6	7	8	9	10
Never		Seldom		Sometimes		Often		Always	

28. I speak up and share from my heart, even when others don't know how to give me the opportunity...

1	2	3	4	5	6	7	8	9	10
Never		Seldom		Sometimes		Often		Always	

29. I act with integrity in my relationships...

1	2	3	4	5	6	7	8	9	10
Never		Seldom		Sometimes		Often		Always	

Section 5
Expanding Love

30. I am responsive to others when they open their hearts & invite me in...

1	2	3	4	5	6	7	8	9	10
Never		Seldom		Sometimes		Often		Always	

31. I take my relationships higher by cherishing others' dreams as well as my own...

1	2	3	4	5	6	7	8	9	10
Never		Seldom		Sometimes		Often		Always	

32. To take relationships higher, I ask even deeper love questions, such as "How loved do you feel today?..."

1	2	3	4	5	6	7	8	9	10
Never		Seldom		Sometimes		Often		Always	

33. I create unity rather than separation in my relationships...

1   2   3   4   5   6   7   8   9   10
Never   Seldom   Sometimes   Often   Always

34. I speak with kindness & honesty flowing as one in my relationships...

1   2   3   4   5   6   7   8   9   10
Never   Seldom   Sometimes   Often   Always

35. I facilitate & champion everyone's right to have equal time to speak, be heard, and feel cherished...

1   2   3   4   5   6   7   8   9   10
Never   Seldom   Sometimes   Often   Always

36. I flow with patience in my relationships...

1   2   3   4   5   6   7   8   9   10
Never   Seldom   Sometimes   Often   Always

37. I express joy & playfulness in my relationships...

1   2   3   4   5   6   7   8   9   10
Never   Seldom   Sometimes   Often   Always

38. I forgive those who have hurt me and I move higher...

1   2   3   4   5   6   7   8   9   10
Never   Seldom   Sometimes   Often   Always

39. I create interdependence, rather than dependency or independence, in my relationships...

1   2   3   4   5   6   7   8   9   10
Never   Seldom   Sometimes   Often   Always

40. I look for ways to empower myself as well as others...

1   2   3   4   5   6   7   8   9   10
Never   Seldom   Sometimes   Often   Always

Section 6
Creating Peace

41. In conflict, I envision the highest possibility of peace before acting...

    1   2   3   4   5   6   7   8   9   10
    Never   Seldom   Sometimes   Often   Always

42. In conflict, I set in motion a *process* to create peace even though there may seem to be no hope for peace...

    1   2   3   4   5   6   7   8   9   10
    Never   Seldom   Sometimes   Often   Always

43. In conflict, I create peace by encouraging others to express feelings openly & with non-violent language...

    1   2   3   4   5   6   7   8   9   10
    Never   Seldom   Sometimes   Often   Always

44 In conflict, I listen with compassion to all sides...

    1   2   3   4   5   6   7   8   9   10
    Never   Seldom   Sometimes   Often   Always

45. In conflict, I treat all parties with unconditional positive regard rather than judgment...

    1   2   3   4   5   6   7   8   9   10
    Never   Seldom   Sometimes   Often   Always

46. In conflict, I am a loving *and* detached observer...

    1   2   3   4   5   6   7   8   9   10
    Never   Seldom   Sometimes   Often   Always

47. In conflict, I express & encourage loving speech...

1   2   3   4   5   6   7   8   9   10
Never   Seldom   Sometimes   Often   Always

48. In conflict, I help get everyone's "story" out in the open & then help them gently move past their story...

1   2   3   4   5   6   7   8   9   10
Never   Seldom   Sometimes   Often   Always

49. In conflict, I help all parties explore solutions for unity and justice...

1   2   3   4   5   6   7   8   9   10
Never   Seldom   Sometimes   Often   Always

50. In conflict, I create gentle, but constant openings for forgiveness...

1   2   3   4   5   6   7   8   9   10
Never   Seldom   Sometimes   Often   Always

51. In conflict, I gently but consistently create peace endings...

1   2   3   4   5   6   7   8   9   10
Never   Seldom   Sometimes   Often   Always

Section 7
Healing With Love

52. I ask Love (or Higher Power) for healing answers...

1   2   3   4   5   6   7   8   9   10
Never   Seldom   Sometimes   Often   Always

53. I bring divine Love's flood of comfort to everyone I know...

1	2	3	4	5	6	7	8	9	10
Never		Seldom		Sometimes		Often		Always	

54. I listen intuitively to Love & let Love (or Higher Power) speak through me to others...

1	2	3	4	5	6	7	8	9	10
Never		Seldom		Sometimes		Often		Always	

55. I call forth the divine in myself & others...

1	2	3	4	5	6	7	8	9	10
Never		Seldom		Sometimes		Often		Always	

56. I offer sweet assurances to my friends & even people I don't know...

1	2	3	4	5	6	7	8	9	10
Never		Seldom		Sometimes		Often		Always	

57. I praise others often & generously...

1	2	3	4	5	6	7	8	9	10
Never		Seldom		Sometimes		Often		Always	

58. I feel Love (or Higher Power) causing me to resonate in harmony with others...

1	2	3	4	5	6	7	8	9	10
Never		Seldom		Sometimes		Often		Always	

59. When faced with problems for myself or others, I hold the space for healing by Love (or Higher Power)...

1	2	3	4	5	6	7	8	9	10
Never		Seldom		Sometimes		Often		Always	

Section 8
Leaving a Trail of Love

(There is only one question in Section 8)

60. When parting from others, I leave a love imprint that uplifts & endures...

1	2	3	4	5	6	7	8	9	10
Never		Seldom		Sometimes		Often			Always

How to Determine Your Love Skills Score

To determine your Love Skills Score, go back and (1) be sure you answered all the questions, (2) add up your total score, and then (3) divide that by 60.

That will give your average **Love Skills Score.** Put that number in the box below and then go to the next page for your **Love Skills Quiz Score Assessment.**

My Average Love Skills Score

Love Skills Score Assessment

Based on your average **Love Skills Score**, find out what this means based on the explanation below. For example, if your score was 7.5, you would read the information below for a "7" and also an "8" since you are in between those two scores.

1. **Sleeping Love Master:** *Not yet birthed* but with all the potential to be a fully awakened Love Master when the awakening begins.

2. **Sleeping Love Master:** *Birthed but still asleep* to the vast potential of a love-filled life. Yet all the treasures of Love remain available.

3. **Novice Love Master:** *Mostly asleep* but not unconscious to the value of love. In great need of a jolt to become a Love Master & begin the journey to higher love ground.

4. **Novice Love Master:** *Just beginning to wake up* with occasional glimpses of the path of love. In need of a catalyst or inner decision to move the energy from sluggishness to waking up.

5. **Emerging Love Master:** *Finding the path of love.* Starting to practice some of the 60 love skills, but just beginning to grasp the potential of what would happen once the love fuse is lit. In great need of a catalyst or inner decision to become a Love Master & begin the journey to higher love ground.

6. **Emerging Love Master:** *Beginning to grasp the possibilities of a love-centered life.* Demonstrating familiarity with many of the 60 love skills – with some significant weaker areas. Capable of making the shift to higher love but in need of significantly more love intention & sustained energy to make it happen.

7. **Practicing Love Master:** *Awakening to the higher possibilities of a love-filled life.* Demonstrating success with many, but not all, of the 60 love skills. Beginning to imagine the possibilities of love. At a crossroads of deciding how high to grow as a Love Master.

8. **Practicing Love Master:** *Wide awake & living a love-centered life.* Demonstrating steady success with almost all 60 love skills. Beginning to taste the vast potential & new dimension of Love beyond this rating scale as the love skills become more and more natural and effortless.

9. **Enlightened Love Master:** *Living in a new dimension of Love beyond any scale or continuum.* Effortlessly expressing & radiating love with almost complete mastery of the 60 love skills. Relying on Love almost exclusively for guidance and dedicated to creating more love everywhere.

10. **Enlightened Love Master:** *Living fully in infinite Love beyond any scale or continuum.* Effortlessly expressing & radiating love with easy mastery of all 60 love skills. Relying on Love exclusively for guidance and dedicated to creating more love throughout the entire universe!

About the Pecks

Scott & Shannon Peck, are passionate about love & teaching & empowering others with love skills that transform relationships & lives.

Scott & Shannon are Love Master teachers, workshop facilitators, speakers, national radio co-hosts, & co-authors of many books on love & healing, including:

- **The Love You Deserve**: *A Spiritual Guide to Genuine Love*
- **Liberating Your Magnificence**
- **Love Skills You Were Never Taught**: *Secrets of a Love Master*
- **Love Heals:** *How to Heal Everything with Love* & *the companion* **Love Heals Study Guide** (both by Shannon Peck)

The Pecks are co-founders of **The Love Center** - www.TheLoveCenter.com - a non-profit educational organization dedicated to *"Raising universal love awareness & awakening a world of Love Masters."*

Shannon Peck is a spiritual healer, author, & teacher of love & healing. Shannon's holds a degree in Religious Studies from Emerson Theological Institute.

Scott Peck earned his Masters Degree in Education & Doctorate in Divinity & has worked professionally as a reporter, photographer, copywriter, educator, national advertising manager, real estate broker, & love teacher.

The Pecks live in San Diego, California.

Contact Us

Please feel free to contact us. We would love to hear what this book has meant to you and how you feel living your life as a Love Master.

Email

ScottandShannonPeck@gmail.com
or
TheLoveCenter@gmail.com

Write

TheLoveCenter
1127 Santa Luisa
Solana Beach, CA 92075

For Lots More Love & Healing Visit

www.TheLoveCenter.com
www.ScottandShannonPeck.com
www.ShannonPeck.com

10833326R00110

Made in the USA
San Bernardino, CA
06 December 2018